AF205831

My Twelve Dates

The author – Corinna Busch

In her book *My Twelve Dates*, former late-night talkshow producer and winner of the Adolf Grimme Award chats light-heartedly about her online dating experiences as a 40-something single woman, but she also talks about her professional life.

In the first part of the book, one chapter is dedicated to each of the 12 dates, and Corinna Busch takes the opportunity to slip in some entertaining anecdotes about celebrities she has worked with over the past 20 years. There's plenty to laugh about.

In the more reflective second part of the book, Corinna consults psychologists about issues that have preoccupied her for many years: Why are dating sites so successful today? Is online dating a playground for narcissists? Can't we find love offline anymore? What can be said about the emotional well-being of society in general? Is the generation of 'war grandchildren' unable to commit to relationships?

In interviews with psychologists Dr Marie-France Hirigoyen and Professor Franz Ruppert, among others, she makes some enlightening and interesting discoveries.

A book that takes a closer look at the phenomenon of online dating.

CORINNA BUSCH

My Twelve Dates

Online Dating, Male Narcissism,
and Other Dramas

There will be men who think they recognise themselves or someone they know in this book. All details, names and descriptions have been changed so that identification is not possible. Similarities with actual persons, living or dead, are purely coincidental: this was not my aim or intention!

Bibliographical Information of the Deutsche Nationalbibliothek:
This publication is listed in the Deutsche Nationalbibliographie of the Deutsche Nationalbibliothek; detailed bibliographical informationcan be accessed under http: //dnb.d-nb.de

© 2020 Corinna Busch
Cover art by newart-graphics/ Shutterstock.com
Printing, Production and Layout:
BoD – Books on Demand, Norderstedt
ISBN 978-3-7504-9123-6

For Bernd and Johanna – somewhere over the rainbow

"This is my true story,
with lies going backward and forward,
because life is often like that"
Olivier Bourdeaut "Waiting for Bojangles"

Foreword

There they were again, my three problems:

40 something, single and not a man in sight!

But how and where do you find the brightest star in the relationship cosmos?

"Try online dating", my friend Susanne suggested one evening. I was so stunned I dropped my Champagne glass. "Are you mad?", I replied. "Only creeps and weirdos use online dating sites. You should know from your own experience."

"Yes", admitted Susi, rolling her eyes, "but it probably works better for blondes. Be strategic about it."

I really didn't understand what Susi meant, and was unsure whether it had to do with the Champagne or the intellectual capacity of a blonde, but after a while, the more I thought about it, the more I liked the idea. I signed up to several dating sites, and set myself the goal of dating 12 men. One of them, surely, would pass muster.

My plan was to sound out candidates first of all on the basis of their nicknames and profile photos. Could "Brown

Sock 67" be the man I'd want to spend the rest of my life with? Or "Desire for more"? Or "Uncle without a roof"? Or maybe "Your tooth fairy"? Then I asked an astrologer to take a look at the candidates and give me his opinion.

Why an astrologer? Well, when you work with as many celebrities as I have in the last 20 years, you experience some interesting, sometimes bizarre situations.

There are some people who even time their showers according to the alignment of the stars. I kid you not! Initially, I was very sceptical about all this star talk. Astrology is something I've never had any great interest in and even today, I'm well aware that natural scientists and astrologers have no common ground. And yet today, many experiences later, I'm convinced that there is sometimes more to astrology than I originally thought.

Eventually, I met the final 12 candidates for real. In this book, you can find out about all the things that happened to me and whether prince charming was among my dates.

Humour helps to heal! This is a view I have shared for many years, and this is why I decided to write humorously about the online dating experiences I had over a period of three years. Although a cheerful person by nature, I didn't always find this easy, because some of the things I experienced with the gentlemen weren't in the least bit funny. However, for me, humour has always been the best way to deal with the many blows of fate that befall us in our lives.

The more extensive my dating experiences became, the more frequently I was confronted with the subject of narcissism and, above all, male narcissism. I began to take a closer look at the subjects of internet dating, narcissism and mental health. I read specialist literature with great interest and consulted different psychologists about these subjects and about mental health in general.

The reflective second part of the book features excerpts from my interviews with these experts. Nobody has the ultimate answer or wants to claim the moral high ground. This section is merely meant to provide food for thought and encourage self-reflection.

I have been interested in psychology for many years, not least of all because of my own background and my professional preoccupation with life coaching. I also spent three years working as a press manager for a group of German clinics specialising in psychological and psychosomatic illnesses.

We face some very great challenges in society today, large parts of which are traumatised. Mental health problems are increasing on an unprecedented scale. This is why I have spent the last few years developing a new project that is so close to my heart. I am delighted that what started out as a vague idea has now become reality. On my website www.my-mentalhealth.com, with the help of experts and celebrities, I will campaign for the de-stigmatisation of mental illness in our traumatised society. I would be delighted if you could find an opportunity to check it out.

I hope you enjoy reading my book. Perhaps you will even gain the occasional insight true to my motto: humour helps to heal!

Corinna Busch

Online Dating, Or:
Are Handbags the Better Men?

We women have a very special relationship with hand-bags. As we do with shoes. Perhaps no emotional bond in a woman's life – with the exception of our bond to chil-dren – is as enduring as our handbag bond. A bold the-ory, I admit, but I know a number of women who would immediately endorse it.

As catwalk coach Bruce Darnell once said:

"Your handbag must be aliiive!"

Whether there's actually life *inside* a woman's handbag is not something I want to go into here. But it's true, I do live *with* my handbag. And maybe my handbag even lives with me, who knows?

I carry around everything but the kitchen sink in my bag – after all, a woman likes to be prepared for all eventu-alities: cosmetics, a fresh set of underwear (tip from a for-mer professional football ref), spare shoes, books, pain-killers, cat food, fabric swatches (for those dresses that are waiting to be designed), a thousand business cards (from people you can't even remember), old plane tickets, scraps of paper with restaurant or hotel names written on them (read about on a flight), perfume samples (that usually stink like hell), boiled sweets from the pharmacy (for emergencies or as food substitutes), and so on ...

Whenever I clear out my handbag (once a year), just

one day later it ends up looking exactly the same as it did before. How *does* she do it?

In a woman's life, handbags have a tendency to multiply in a rather uncanny way. They approach you. Quietly. Purring.

You stand there in front of a store display, admiring these magnificent specimens. They have names like 'Bella Donna' or 'Principessa' and they whisper to you imploringly: "Go on, you want me too. Take me! I'm a bargain! I'm the answer to your sleepless nights."

My experiences with internet dating followed a similar pattern. I'd sit in front of my computer and the men on offer, or men who were offering themselves, had names. So-called profile names. Typically, the gentlemen claimed to be down-to-earth. They called themselves "Ready for love" (high time too at 56), "No roof over my head" (probably kicked out by the wife), "Hot chocolate man" (visits Mum every Sunday for her home-baked cakes), or "Verbal gymnast" (talks non-stop during sex and loves long, convoluted sentences).

I'd been single for some time, and to be honest, didn't believe in online dating. But my offline endeavours hadn't produced much in the way of suitable candidates either.

What did men use to do when they admired or loved a woman? Lots of crazy, wonderful things. They threw roses out of helicopters or renounced a kingdom. They bought diamonds the size of a football or had pre-warmed cushions placed on their beloved's chair in restaurants.

What do men do today? They write WhatsApp messages!

Do you know members of the WhatsApp generation? These are people who live by virtue of and with electronic media. They have relationships on WhatsApp, Tinder or other online platforms. It's convenient, avoids real intimacy and – oops, apparently it does happen – they can date multiple people simultaneously.

A while ago I met a man. It all started off with us sending each other WhatsApp messages, as is customary these days. Our first real meeting took place weeks later. It then turned out that the man was not – as he'd assured me in writing beforehand – single, but that he still lived with his wife. Emotionally, though, he claimed they had separated *aaaages* ago. He was just waiting for the right moment to pack his cases.

In other words, a lot of wives and partners have no idea that in reality they're single – and have been for years!

Unfortunately, I'd fallen for the man and suddenly found myself in the WhatsApp trap again. The man was incredibly busy – and surprise, surprise, had little or no time to meet up, but he continued to text me. It was so nice and convenient.

When I was ill and confined to bed, there were no visits, no flowers, no chocolates. Nothing. Any concern was expressed via WhatsApp message. Then the man promptly disappeared out of my life just as he had entered it: by WhatsApp! He had no time to talk to me personally.

The sad truth of the matter is I know a lot of very similar stories.

How damaged must the male brain be for a man to behave like this?? Courting, making an effort to get to know a woman 'offline', in real life, sadly seems to have gone entirely out of fashion. Whatever happened to chivalry?

I rounded up some of my friends, both male and female, and during a long, amusing inaugural meeting, we decided to set up a new group:

The DROP DEAD WhatsApp –WeWantMenWhoTake-UsInTheirArmsAndShowerUsWithRoses group.

We decided that BEFORE a first date, the male candidate should be asked to provide the following:

1. a divorce certificate, original copy, or
2. a notarised separation agreement or declaration of intent
3. a certificate attesting to successful participation in an etiquette course on manners, courtesy, and general good behaviour
4. the names of three guarantors who can be interviewed about the candidate by phone beforehand in order to ascertain which shortcomings to expect and under what circumstances
5. a bag full of gifts – as a gesture of goodwill.

And so, with my romantic situation not looking especially rosy in the 'offline' world, I thought, why not? Why not try my luck online? Maybe I was wrong to have so many prejudices and reservations about cyber-dating.

Based on the principle that 'a little is good, more is better', I signed up to three different dating sites. I uploaded two or three photos of myself and wrote some halfway entertaining profile texts. My personal motto was the same on all platforms: "Never eat yellow snow!"

Then it was a question of waiting. A couple of days later, when I checked my inboxes, I nearly fell off my chair with surprise. I had received over 300 responses! How on earth was I ever going to read them all? Even worse, how could I meet them all? How could I narrow down my choice?

I'd initially planned to date 13 men, but was then unsure about the number. I turned to my astrologer Merlin for advice.

"Thirteen men? Mmmm … what about 12? You could write about them too!"

He chuckled. I glanced at him sideways and had to laugh.

"Are the stars favourable for a book?"

Merlin nodded.

"Why not write a bit about your life? You've had so many bizarre experiences with so many celebrities!"

Even though I really am interested in astrology, I don't plan my everyday life around it. My astrological passion doesn't go that far, but I am convinced, for instance, that certain star signs are a good match, while others aren't. For example, as a Sagittarius, I usually get on well with Aries and Leo. Pisces and Capricorn, too. I was born with the moon in Libra, so Libras are also a pretty good match for me. Taurus and Scorpios are more of a problem. Virgos can sometimes be a challenge too.

"Okay, I'll get started. Again, how many should I meet?"

Merlin stroked the non-existent hair on his head and said:

"Twelve's a good number. It reflects the diversity of creation. The number 12 has so many meanings. It's one of the most magical numbers – it symbolises perfection, there are 12 signs of the zodiac, 12 months in a year, the moon orbits the Earth 12 times."

Indeed, why not date 12 men? A dozen dates. That was it! Merlin offered to give me an astrological assessment of the men based on their profile pictures, nicknames and dates of birth before each of my 12 dates.

I'd already decided on three different types of meeting: breakfast/coffee date (for the weak candidates), lunch dates (for the halfway interesting men) and dinner dates (for the hot guys).

In the first round, I focused only on profile pictures and headlines, placing 100 candidates I considered to be attractive in a file. One of them made it into my pre-selection list on the basis of the professional networking site link he added to his subject line. Then I started reading.

Unfortunately, there were a lot of incredibly dull messages among the e-mails. Most of them didn't get much further than a "Hello, blonde lady, nice picture. How are you?". Sobering to say the least.

Dear Gentlemen, have you never heard of that famous 'first sentence'? Doesn't it ring any bells? In books, for example, opening lines can be crucial in terms of whether or not someone purchases a book. If they don't immediately grab attention, potential buyers are far more likely to put the book back on the shelf again. Reject. Adios.

I spent months deliberating on what the first sentence in this book would be. Then one day, there it was! I think it's important how a conversation starts. But what is a good first sentence? The answer is shockingly simple: the first sentence should arouse interest in the second, and then the third.

In online dating, the first sentence should arouse my interest in a person. It should open up a door to someone I don't yet know and ask me to come inside. A first sentence, for example, should NOT invite me to share bodily fluids.

Here are the three worst first sentences I read:

1. 0176 / 12 34 56 xxx
2. Hi Cora, do you like 3? *(meaning, I assume, a threesome)*
3. Regina, do you have WhatsApp?

If the profile picture was not an absolute cracker and the first sentence uninspiring, I immediately pressed delete. Progress had to be made somehow. Then I wrote to the

12 finalists and suggested we met in person. With some of the candidates, my proposal prompted an enthusiasm I found hard to fathom. They seemed especially needy. Then the messaging back and forth began.

But which of the 12 gentlemen should I date first? I wrote down each of the nicknames on a piece of paper, screwed them up and then tossed them all in the air. (I'm sure this could be the subject of deeper psychological analysis, but I'll skip that bit). Then I picked the first piece of paper out of the pile.

1. Date: Wild Rider

On the paper, I read:

Wild Rider (52 years old, Taurus, Libra rising)

Almost two metres tall, this giant-of-a-man could hardly be overlooked. He had short-cropped brown hair, a slightly longish face and friendly-looking brown eyes. There was something weighty about him that wasn't just to do with his round belly, but generally he had a pleasant demeanour. He worked in the financial department of a public authority.

Before our date, my first online candidate wrote extensively about his enthusiasm for me (wherever that came from). Hans wrote his heart out and looked forward to our meeting with eager anticipation.

I unexpectedly had to go abroad on a business trip and Hans could barely wait for me to return. He'd evidently discovered both my blog and my affinity to France:

Corinna, I'm totally "bouleversée" with excitement. A funny, creative, attractive woman (the order is intended and based on priority) whose vocabulary and enjoyment of our language is so appealing – You don't find that very often!

I just called the airline and asked the pilot to "go full throttle" on your return flight. So don't be surprised if the flight's short. I'll arrange to meet you at the airport.

If we meet, I promise you I won't give a damn about the restaurant or the menu. The only thing that matters to me is that you wear the hot shoes that adorned your pretty little feet in your concert photo. I'd be so speechless I wouldn't be able to tell you much about myself. I would ravish you with my eyes and just let you eat. Or maybe you'll let me talk you into going for a ride with me. Our first date in rubber boots, how does that sound? The only problem would be the restaurant, because I'd have to reserve extra tables for the horses.

Best wishes, Hans

Hans wrote me messages like this every day. There was often something unintentionally comical about them, and this amused me.

Thanks for your kind wishes. I really need them. The horses and dogs have been digging up the entire paddock since yesterday.

I've just registered with an online vegetarian group and signed up for the next meal. I'm doing so with an open-minded curiosity. I had no idea you can eat plants, and I can't wait to see what vegetarians make of a passionate meat-eater like. I wonder how tolerant they are ;-)))))

But enough of that, I'll let you get on with your breakfast. Oh, by the way, please don't go and emigrate on me before we've even met. Depending on how our meeting goes, I might even sponsor it ;-)))

Yours, Hans

The last sentence perplexed me a little. What did he mean? Did he want to send me abroad if he found me obnoxious? Or did he want to emigrate with me if romance was in the air?

It was time to ask my dear astrologer friend Merlin what he made of this "I-go-to-vegetarian-meetings-even-though-I'm-a-meat-eater" man.

Merlin lives in his own astrological world. Visually, he cuts a striking and imposing figure: bald, never without a hat, always flamboyantly dressed.

Merlin entered Hans' date of birth into the astrology programme on his computer and then stared for several minutes at the generated horoscope. He grunted occasionally and his eyes opened wide. I don't know to this day what goes through his head when he looks at a person's horoscope for the first time.

He fidgeted around on his chair and stroked his head over and over again. Is this where information from the universe was arriving? I have no idea. One thing I have learned in the many years of our friendship though is that nobody else can describe or analyse characters and biographies on the basis of their horoscope and pictures as accurately as he can. It's almost uncanny.

Then Merlin made his pronouncements:

"So with the position of the sun like this ... he has a problem. How should I put it ... he often misjudges situations. The man is quite a unique character, someone who always manages to somehow muddle through. In a Western, he'd be the person researching butterflies. While the cowboys and Indians are shooting and fighting each other, he'd be in the midst of it all chasing butterflies with his net. He'd remain unscathed. The Indians would let him wander around – a source of amusement to all.

Ultimately though, he's a kind of tragic figure with rather low self-esteem."

This also fit in with the many quirky messages Hans had written me.

"He's practically born with a talent for psychology which he could use to treat himself. He's also interested in understanding the mystifications of life which he is caught up in. He has three planets in the eighth house, in other words in depth psychology, he is condemned by fate, as it were, to preoccupy himself with his psyche."

I told Merlin about an earlier burnout Hans had mentioned in one of his messages. After what he referred to as a "brief period of painting therapy", however, he had reverted to his old routine without gaining any significant new insights. Merlin nodded.

"His Venus is in your rising sign. I think he'll find you pretty hot."

Merlin laughed.

"I hope you have an enjoyable time."

Hans suggested we met at a hotel bar "because it's the perfect place for your shoes", he claimed. I didn't immediately grasp the causal connection between my Manolo Blahniks and this hotel bar, but then again, men and high heels are a story in their own right. If a woman drops a scarf, for example, the chances a man will pick it up are 50 percent higher if the woman is wearing heels. I didn't want to be a spoilsport so I agreed to his proposal. Shame on whoever thinks evil of a man who suggests a hotel bar for a first date ... But Hans' unintentional humour had won me over.

Just in case we still liked each other after our aperitif, Hans planned to book a table at an Italian restaurant close to the hotel.

Despite rush-hour traffic and wintery conditions, I arrived at the hotel bar almost on time, only to be confronted with – Goliath! Goodness, the man was tall! Greeting first his breast pockets, I ignored the pain radiating from a herniated disc and craned my neck upwards so that I could look him in the eye.

Hans seemed a little tense.

"I've been waiting here for you for half an hour. I've already downed my first glass of wine."

Alarmed, I flinched a little.

"Did I get the time wrong? Didn't we say 7 pm? You know, blondes have a bit of a problem with dates and times."

Hans laughed.

"No, I was just nervous and afraid of turning up late. Do you have so many dates? Do you meet lots of men? But come and sit down first! The Christmas decorations are already up, isn't that nice?"

Reluctant to tell Hans about my multiple dating experiments, I launched into an explanation about the challenges of being blonde.

"Hans, you have no idea – why should you, you have brown hair! – how many dates a blonde woman has! It's bizarre. A blonde woman's day is filled with appointments. Sometimes, I have trouble getting everything done in 24 hours. I've given up sleeping. Hans, even my car has appointments. It's incredible."

Hans looked at me slightly perplexed, pushing back his chair slightly. I think he found me rather scary.

"Okay, your car has appointments. Interesting. What kind? Do you drive a lot?"

"I enjoy driving my old car, yes. Well, when you can actually drive. On German roads you spend most of your time in traffic jams. Do you know, recently a radio station tried to find a different word for 'traffic jam' to make the endless traffic warnings a bit more interesting. Listeners were asked to suggest alternatives. They came up with made-up words like as 'bumper tango' or 'car clogging'."

"Wow, interesting ..."

The man had difficulties following my flow.

"Do you know what my favourite suggestion was?"

Additional wrinkles appeared on Hans' forehead and he looked at me expectantly.

"What was your favourite word?"

"'Time for me!' Isn't that GREAT?! On the A59, from Cologne to Oberhausen, 15 kilometres of 'time for me'. So I spend all my time in the car – because that's where I FINALLY have time for myself! It's a completely new feeling."

"Oh, I'll have to try that out myself. Time for me and the dogs. Maybe I won't get so uptight when I'm driving."

"But we were really talking about my car's appointments."

"Right, that's how you started. So what appointments does your car have?"

"So in July, when it was 29 degrees, the guy at my garage called me and said: Ms Busch, you really are a true blonde! It's 29 degrees and you're still driving around with your winter tires. Come to the garage NOW!"

Hans burst out laughing, almost choking on his wine.

"I went straight to my car to cool down the tires with some ice-cubes. Then I drove to the garage. The day before yesterday, there was an envelope from the garage guy in my letter box. The note inside had only two words on it: "Winter tires"!

Hans was so tickled he could hardly contain himself, giving me the chance to take a closer look at Goliath. Opposite me sat a pleasant-looking man with a slightly rustic appearance. His outfit had clearly seen better days and his clunky shoes were still caked with mud from his paddock.

We were sitting on two bar stools and Hans had problems arranging his long legs under the glass table. Every time he tried to cross them his knee lifted the tabletop by around 50 centimetres. He shrugged with embarrassment.

"Bit of a squeeze here," he mumbled.

I couldn't stop myself from giggling and to my relief Hans shared my amusement. The unintended humour of his messages continued when we met. The man *was* unique, Merlin was absolutely right.

Hans, in the meantime, had ordered me a glass of Champagne and we raised our glasses to each other. Goliath shared his toast with half the bar:

"Prost, Corinna. Sober I'm shy, but smashed I'm a sensation!"

Oh boy, what a delightful prospect that was! I knew even before this toast that Hans would not be accompanying me on the journey through the rest of my life. So I was able to smile at his funny, sometimes coarse comments.

When I asked him when he'd split up from his previous partner, he hummed and hawed:

"Well, umm … I haven't moved out yet, but I will soon."

"Ah, that's interesting. Does your wife actually know you want to move out?"

I leant back on my bar chair, eager to hear Hans' response.

"Well, she probably guesses, but we haven't actually talked about it yet. If I'd written to you that I was still married, you'd never have met me. I swear, I did feel guilty doing it."

Hans sat opposite me looking rather dejected and he ordered another glass of wine.

"I feel truly sorry for your wife. What a nasty piece of work you are!"

"I don't like myself sometimes either. But I don't physically desire my wife any more. She's too fat and too old, I just can't help it. There are so many attractive younger women on the internet. There's such a huge choice."

"Hans, have you ever looked in the mirror? You're overweight and not exactly a spring chicken yourself. What do you expect? You obviously need this for your own male ego. In my experience, you're not the only one either. Are you men all a bit disturbed?"

Hans spoke about his wife without any feeling of compassion, admitting to me he had signed up to multiple online dating platforms and was dating several women simultaneously. He said it boosted his ego. While he was telling me this, I tried to examine my own feelings.

His unintentional humour initially drew me to him, made me find him amusing. But then there was the self-ish way he treated his wife, and she wasn't the only one he cheated on. Part of his personality seemed to me to be troubled and in need of treatment. He was constantly in search of self-affirmation and his next sexual 'kick'.

He even showed me a piece of paper on which he documented his current 'dating status'. Written down were the names of ten women, their ages, professions, family status and distance from his home. He wrote to all of them simultaneously, many of them he had already met – and in some cases had sex with.

"The note is important so that I don't get them mixed up. For example, I don't want to ask Uschi about her daughter if she hasn't got any children, mixing her up with Martina."

I thanked him for the aperitif and headed home.

2. Date: BritPop

So my first date had been a blast. I was already on the verge of giving up. There were still eleven more men on my list. How on earth was I going to survive them if they were all as disastrous as the first?

I decided to put on a brave face and rise to the challenge.

BritPop (48 years old, Aries, Leo rising)

From his profile picture, BritPop was certainly an attractive man, not unlike the actor Hugh Grant. Dark brown, slightly wavy hair, a friendly, open smile. In his photo he wore a tailored shirt and jacket and he looked generally very neat, perhaps a bit on the stiff side. His forehead was high, his aura smart.

I visited Merlin in his astrologer's cave and asked him to give me an astrological assessment of my next dating candidate.

"Well, he has four planets in Aries, so he's an Aries through and through. An Aries has no past. What just happened is done and dusted. If someone shakes your hand but doesn't look you in the eye when you're saying goodbye, this is most probably an Aries. For him, you're already passé.

Your candidate here contradicts everyone and everything, even himself. This means he's always right. Unfortunately, his sun is positioned at a rather catastrophic point, at 27 degrees, with Saturn in Aries."

Merlin exhaled from his inflated cheeks. I had no idea what that meant and looked at him questioningly.

"Is he perverse? Shouldn't I meet him?"

Merlin almost fell off his chair laughing.

"No, he's not perverse. But when the sun is at this degree, life isn't going to be easy. This is how the stars were aligned one day after the sinking of the Titanic."

I looked at Merlin as blankly as apparently only a dumb blonde can look. What did Mr. BritPop have to do with the sinking of the Titanic?

"It's simply a disaster point. This is a highly intelligent, very scientifically-minded man, a titan of the mind, and by extension, he is the Titanic. He is so brilliant he has to be careful not to overdo things and sink. He has a tendency to expect too much of himself and be overly ambitious. He's a very interesting guy, but there's something dogged about him. Let's put it this way: he takes one step forward, and then one step back again. Sadly, there are more and more relationships that live only in the past, which means they have no future. Most end up where they started – separately."

This fascinated me and was consistent with the experiences I'd had myself in the past few years.

"Why do you think it's becoming more and more difficult to have a happy relationship?"

"The world is in a state of disarray and more and people are losing all sense of perspective. Everyone is born with a certain perspective that suits them. But many have lost this. A lot of people consider themselves to be incredibly important and irreplaceable. They lose themselves in their own self-indulgence. Virtually no one thinks systemically anymore. There is a tendency towards 'over-individualisation'.

The team is usually the star, but nowadays we humans all want to be the star ourselves. This applies in relationships, too. There is also the emancipation of women, who have had enough of the last few centuries. And rightly so. Men today often have a problem with that."

I was truly curious to meet the titanic Aries.

Born and raised in Manchester, Stephan wrote only short, matter-of-fact messages. Occasionally, a hint of the famous British black humour slipped through, and I liked that. There were no virtual kisses or roses. The man was rather straightforward, but I liked that too. All that "you're the woman of my dreams", all those hearts and kisses from men I'd never even met made my skin crawl.

Stephan might even have been a dinner candidate if it hadn't been for the fact that he was only free at lunchtime during the week, supposedly because of stress at work. This should have been a warning. He'd only mentioned in passing that he no longer lived with his wife and three children.

We arranged to meet for lunch at a little Italian place. I'd stupidly made a note of the wrong time and turned up at the restaurant half an hour early. I found a nice table, ordered a drink and then started reading the memoirs of psychoanalyst and author Irvin Yalom, whom I admire greatly.

A short while later, a dark-haired, middle-aged man entered the restaurant and sat down at a table opposite me. When the waiter asked him what he'd like to drink, the guest said he was waiting for someone.

A few minutes later, a woman in her mid-30s arrived carrying a bouquet of flowers. She was dressed from head to toe in black. I simply couldn't help it – I had to put down Irvin and eavesdrop the conversation at the table next to me.

Smiling hesitantly, the man got up and approached her.
"Oh, am I a girl?"

The woman: "Come again?"

The man: "Because of the flowers."

She handed him the flowers and embraced him.

"Yes, they're your birthday present."

Slightly perturbed, the man took the flowers and looked at her.
"Oh, thanks. Yes, flowers. For me."

The couple sat down and ordered a bottle of water.

The woman: "Well, you know, actually I bought you a plant for your roof terrace. But then I re-potted it yesterday evening. I put it in one of my terracotta pots. It looked so nice that I decided to keep it. And I bought you the flowers instead."

He looked annoyed. She drank water.

The man: "Would you like an aperitif? A glass of *Sekt* maybe?"

The woman: "Yes, *Sekt* would be nice. Although maybe something with a bit of colour *(glancing at her clothes, I got that)*. A spritz, or whatever it's called."

The man: "You mean an Aperol? Yes, that's a nice colour."

The woman: "Yes, that's right. So, how old are you now?"

The man: "Fifty."

The woman: "Oh dear."

He looked perplexed.

The woman: "Well, maybe you'll live to a ripe old age."

The man: "Yes, I'll have a healthy lunch. I'll order a salad so that I live to be 100. That means I'm only half way through my life today. Not such a bad prospect."

She took a large gulp of Aperol spritz.

The man: "I think a lot about life these days. I was baptised a Christian, but I find Buddhism interesting too. I'm part of nature and part of something."

The woman: "I don't understand a word you're saying. What do you mean?"

The man: "It's fascinating. Our matter and all the nuclear waste. Will we all end up in a big black hole?"

She continued drinking her Aperol spritz *(probably still not understanding a word he said).*

The man: "So what shall we eat? I really might have a salad. The one with prawns. You know I can't eat whole animals – I have scruples about that."

The woman: "I need another Aperol."

Just as I started pinching myself to contain my laughter, Stephan arrived.

Politely, he stretched out his hand in greeting, smiling shyly. This really was Hugh Grant's younger brother standing opposite me. Physically at least. Brown, slightly wavy hair, well-cut suit. Black – probably hand-stitched – brogues. There was a classiness about Stephan. He could have come straight from an Oxford University lecture.

Right from the start, I was bothered by his eyes. Very attractive deep blue eyes with long, thick lashes. Somehow, though, they were lifeless. I saw no joy in them.

The man struck me as being emotionally remote and it was difficult to get a conversation going. I still had to stifle my laughter. The conversation I'd overheard at the next table was simply priceless.

Stephan noticed I couldn't stop smiling and obviously didn't have a clue what it was all about. Not wanting him to think my shaking shoulders had something to do with him, I leaned across the table and tried explaining to him in whispered sentences about the conversation I'd overheard. Unfortunately, he didn't share my amusement and continued to be somehow reserved and aloof.

I encouraged him to tell me a little bit about himself.

"Well, there's not much to tell. I grew up in Manchester and studied medicine in the States. My parents split up when I was young, so I spent several years at boarding school in England. After I finished my degree, I started working for a firm in New York that finds venture capital for pharmaceutical companies."

He told me how he'd helped several pharmaceutical companies develop new medication and look for investors. He'd sold his own company for a big profit a few years previously and didn't really need to work anymore, but he continued to slog away like a man possessed.

Stephan sat very straight on his chair, eating his spaghetti carbonara deliberately. Each strand of spaghetti was twisted slowly and carefully around his fork. There was something almost devout about it. I got the impression that my naturally cheerful disposition had somehow overwhelmed him and I began to suspect that a stick had been implanted next to his backbone and was making his life altogether rather difficult.

And then he blurted it out. He wasn't yet properly separated from his wife and three children – they were apart only during the week. At the weekends, he returned to the family home. But he was on the verge of really separating, he'd been thinking about it for a long time. It couldn't go on like this anymore.

Sure, of course. Was I only ever going to meet men who wanted a little bit of comfort and variety in their lives from Mondays to Thursdays? Why can't men sort out their private lives and separate from partners in an orderly, amicable fashion OR simply steer clear of dating sites and <u>not</u> put a cross next to 'Looking for a new relationship'?

"Why on earth did you write to me?", I asked, annoyed.

"I liked your pictures and you have such positive energy."

I didn't appreciate this well-meant compliment and felt seriously cheated. Sadly, this date also ended rather abruptly and I left the man to get on with the rest of his life.

That same evening, I called an emergency meeting with Susi, Merlin and our mutual friend René. We met in a shabby Argentinian restaurant that served pizza and baked potatoes, but not a single steak dish. The wood-panelled joint hadn't changed in 25 years but we loved the warm hospitality and the excellent pizza. This was where every fortnight the four of us held our 'socio-politically significant gatherings'.

"I've already had it up to here! Really, I've had enough. There are only weirdos out there."

René patted my hand across the table, trying to calm me down:

"Sweetheart, stay cool. Let's have a glass of bubbly and then everything will look different," he purred in his own inimitable manner that probably only a gay ballet master can get away with.

I looked at him sceptically but had to laugh. I picked up the glass of Champagne René had ordered me and raised it to my friends. We bad-mouthed all the evil men in the world and had a blast.

That evening, I had no idea that my next date was going to throw me completely off track ...

3. Date: Fabrice

My next date had two qualities that automatically pro-pelled him to the top of my ranking list: one, he was French, two, he was a musician in a chamber orchestra.

What a fantastic combination! My friends know only too well how enthusiastic I am about all things French, and music has played an important role in my life ever since I was a child.

Then there was the fact that Fabrice looked fantastic. Slim, tall and elegant, slightly wavy black hair, long, slen-der hands – and 14 years younger than me. Now THAT was something that stopped me in my tracks.

What did a man want from a woman who was so much older? Equally, what did I want from a younger man? Given my predilection for always choosing the rather unconventional route through life, however, plus the fact that this whole fuss about age is irrelevant anyway (except for when it comes to a bottle of wine), I decided to dismiss the matter.

Fabrice (34 years old, Libra, Libra rising)

Looking at his profile picture, Merlin was evidently blown away by the Frenchman's physical attributes.

"Holy cow, what a hunk! Look at the way he's standing there with his clarinet – like a mini Macron. What can I say? He's a gifted musician. Libra rising, the sun in Libra and in the twelfth house, the moon in Cancer, so in your Ascendant. You'll definitely hit it off at first, in any case."

Merlin grinned.

"He's all about music, music, music. The pair of you together could be an explosion of fireworks, lightning will
strike – When they met, the Gods cast lightning! The at-
traction could be so strong, you might be afraid of getting
your fingers burnt."

Now, if that wasn't a promising perspective! I became
increasingly curious about Fabrice. Where there's light,
however, there's shadow.

"The young man is popular with the ladies and he's extremely ambitious. Music is his life and he'll find it hard
to commit to a real relationship. It would take a lot for
that to happen. On no account does he want to jeopardise
his career.

  If he really abandoned himself to a woman, he'd feel
he was losing control, being reckless. The life of a professional musician in a classical orchestra requires a lot of
discipline. Under no circumstances does he want to lose
his freedom. But true love is a commitment. He likes love,
but not the price of love – the commitment."

I couldn't wait to meet Fabrice. The young man was
clearly a dinner candidate, but unfortunately he was in
the middle of a series of concerts, which put paid to that
idea. So we arranged to meet for lunch. He usually had
orchestra rehearsal in the mornings, and couldn't yet say
when he'd be free. One day before our date, a text arrived
from Fabrice:

"Hello madame, I can maybe come a little earlier tomorrow, I'll see. Are you still flexible?"

I liked the French way he wrote. What German man would call you madame? Wonderful!

"Hello Fabrice, yes, I'm still flexible tomorrow. No problem."

"Okay, I'll let you know tomorrow. One o'clock should be good. How are you otherwise?"

"Thanks, Fabrice, I'm fine. I hope you are too?"

"Mais oui, I'm good."

I couldn't help smiling and was excited about the following day. Fabrice texted me again a couple of hours before we were due to meet:

"One o'clock is good. Rehearsals are finished. How much time do you have?"

"I'm easy, I have no appointments this afternoon."

"Oh good, madame. I have an appointment in Dortmund in the afternoon. Let's meet in the restaurant, okay?"

"Great. See you in a bit."

We both arrived outside the Italian restaurant at exactly the same time.

He approached from one direction, I came from the other. Quite an achievement.

Fabrice wore black glasses and his beard was longer than in the photos, but it didn't make him any less attractive. He was without doubt an exceptionally good-looking man, tall and elegantly turned-out. He wore a beige, slim-fit overcoat, dark trousers and a black shirt and black, well-polished leather shoes.

He opened the door to the restaurant for me (extra marks) and we looked for a quiet corner. After we'd decided what to drink (still water) and what to eat (pasta with veal Bolognese and truffle), we sat there staring at each other for what felt like ten minutes. There was a certain feeling between us I found hard to put my finger on. Light, tingly, yet natural. As though we knew each other, but were only just getting to know each other.

"Do you know Lang Lang?"

I looked at him with wide eyes and began laughing

"Why do you ask?"

"I saw the photo of him with you on your charity website. I'm a musician too, so I thought that was interesting. I played with him once in a concert."

I remembered the photo. So Fabrice had evidently been looking through my old charity website 'Stargebot'. When I set up Stargebot in 2007, it was the first charity auction platform in Germany. Celebrities could auction off personal items or a slot of their personal time for a good cause. The proceeds went to various charity organisations. Lang Lang auctioned a personal meeting after one of his concerts and the auction winner was delighted with his prize.

"I did a project with Lang Lang a long time ago. He's a really nice guy", I answered, satisfying Fabrice's curiosity.

"Do you spend a lot of time with celebrities?"

"Not any more. It became too exhausting in the end."

I winked at Fabrice and took a sip of water.

"Why exhausting? Are all celebrities exhausting? Je comprehends pas."

I had to laugh.

"No, they're not all exhausting. Let's say the really successful ones are rarely exhausting. They're usually pretty laid-back. The less successful ones sometimes think they're the centre of the universe and THAT can be exhausting ...! The partners of successful people can be exhausting too. Sometimes they behave as though they're the celebrities, not their husband or wife. I've had some bizarre experiences. For example, one client of mine wanted more media coverage. When he got married, he didn't ask his best friend to be the best man at his wedding, he asked a famous musician. He wanted his wedding photos to be in the press at all costs and the musician's presence at the wedding attracted a lot of attention in the media."

Fabrice looked at me stunned, rolled his brown eyes and started laughing.

"I see. That would drive me mad. You must have a lot of patience and strong nerves."

Sitting opposite me was a very smart man.

In the meantime, plates of truly delicious tagliatelle had been brought to our table but our meal didn't interrupt the flow of our conversation. Do you know that feeling? When the words just roll effortlessly off your tongue? Your entire body swings with the conversation, almost like a melody? Fabrice talked about his life as a musician. He'd sometimes despaired as a student and on two occasions had almost thrown it all in.

"I was convinced I couldn't do it. I was about to lose myself. I just felt I wasn't performing at my full potential. I practiced like mad, but was never satisfied. Then one day, everything just fell into place. Things got easier and I eventually managed to finish my degree."

Time just flew by. After a quick espresso, Fabrice had to leave. We said goodbye to each other outside the restaurant and there was mention of another meeting.

The next morning he sent me a text asking if he could take me out to dinner. I was delighted.

Three days later, there we sat in a French restaurant, drinking Champagne and eating our way through half the menu.

"Madame, in your presence I feel destabilised," Fabrice murmured in that delightful French accent.

I, too, felt slightly destabilised and wasn't sure if it had to do with the Champagne or Fabrice. For my own stabilisation, I promptly ordered another glass. We had an exhilarating evening together and in the background violins played.

Were the Gods unleashing lightning on us, as Merlin had predicted? Maybe they were warming up before delivering the ultimate strike ... There was tension in the air. We were certainly taken by each other, and there was a mutual fascination. But it bothered Fabrice, because he wasn't – as he'd already admitted – ready for a serious relationship. He wanted to have fun, and I understood that. He hadn't expected to feel so "destabilised" in my presence. C'est la vie.

Fabrice left on a concert tour with his orchestra for several weeks and we both agreed the distance would be good for us. We liked each other too much for a quick fling. And in any case, I wasn't interested in having a casual affair. I was through with that.

We stayed in touch for a while, and sometimes I still go to his concerts.

4. Date: GourmetSnob

My next experiment brought me back to German man.

GourmetSnob (51 years old, Scorpio, Leo rising)

Looking at his profile picture, I decided that physically this man was certainly no knockout – but there was something about him. Short black hair, a distinctive, lined face (no signs of any Botox excesses here, thank goodness), a deeply furrowed brow. I imagined him being very smart. He was a manager with an insurance company. His eyes had a slightly mocking expression, but he didn't seem disagreeable. He appealed to me. There were signs of chubbiness and a double chin, but all within limits. And I liked his message:

"Hello, young lady, your picture looks somehow familiar. Is it possible there was an article about you in a women's magazine? (good first sentence, yes, that's possible.) *I don't usually read that kind of thing* (nooo, of course not)*, but it's a funny coincidence! Do you know the restaurant Luzy Wang?* (I knew the restaurant.) *It used to be my extended living room (mine too). I was there again recently .... the duck!!!!* (He apparently meant he liked eating their Asian duck. As did I.) *I'd like to take you out to dinner there. Shall we text to arrange the details?"*

The man had mentioned a difficult medium for me, but at least he didn't beat about the bush (meeting), and arrangements had to be made somehow. But dinner? I didn't find him that hot. Eventually, I persuaded him to agree to a lunch date.

Merlin didn't give me much hope either.

"He has an interesting personality. There's a slight chauvinism that comes from Leo, and a tendency to show off. He might be in love with himself.
His sun is in Cancer, your Ascendant. Scorpio and Cancer are always attracted to each other and both of your Moon signs are in Libra."

Merlin laughed. I wasn't sure whether I should look forward to a date with this interesting character or not. However, Merlin had more messages from 'above'.

"This candidate is secrecy himself. Mister Ominous. He likes to distract attention away from things with his mischievous manner. He's a smooth operator, a highly intelligent man and his word is law. He's a gifted problem-solver – sometimes solving problems he's created himself. He can be incredibly charming and has a great affinity with music and culture. Have an enjoyable time."

GourmetSnob and I arrived at Luzy Wang the same time, which I took to be a good sign. But somehow, from the word go, my manager date seemed a little annoyed. As it happened, the restaurant chef Titzu didn't only know him well, but – tadaa – yours truly too, and it was me he first welcomed with a big, friendly hug.

My date stood next to me with his nose slightly out of joint.

"You know each other?"

Titzu and I both nodded.

Michael alias GourmetSnob was evidently accustomed to being the first in the restaurant to receive a personal welcome from the chef. After we'd finally found a table we both liked, we eyed each other extensively. There was something comical about the situation. I had to laugh.

"Why are you laughing?"

Michael gave me a sideways glance, but couldn't help smiling too. In true executive manager style, he placed two iPhones on the table, probably to prove to himself just how important he was.

Every so often, he glanced with raised eyebrows at the two displays, casually answering incoming messages while we were talking. This didn't earn him any bonus points. If I hadn't been looking forward to a delicious Asian meal so much, I would have got up and left.

Why do people have to put phones on the table in restaurants, spending more time looking at their screens than at their companions? It's a dreadful trend.

For me, there are only two acceptable reasons why anyone should have their phone out during dinner: either because their kids are sick and the babysitter might sound the alarm at any moment, or someone is dying. In any other case, employers and social media sites can surely cope if phones are switched off for a couple of hours or, even better, left at home!

Visibly nervous, Michael was doing his best to appear cool and casual. A colourful scarf was wrapped around his neck, his shirt strained across a bulging belly, and tight-fitting trousers meant that dessert was completely out of the question. His stylishness somehow looked pretentious.

"I usually drink a Spanish red wine here, but I won't at lunchtime," announced my date, ordering a large bottle of water "without bubbles", as he put it.

"So, here we are. All rather strange."

Michael grinned.

"So tell me, you wrote that you used to work in the German Chancellery. How did that come about?"

I don't know how often I've been asked this question in the last few years, and inwardly I rolled my eyes. Not wanting to snub my date after only five minutes, however, I smiled at him and pretended there was nothing I'd like to talk about more.

"Oh, it's a funny story. At the end of the 1980s, there weren't enough apprenticeships and training programmes in Germany, so Helmut Kohl decided the German Chancellery should do its bit and train more young people".

I told him a little more about my time there.

"I was about to finish school and was trying to decide what to do afterwards – go straight to university or do a trainee programme? And if so, what kind of a programme? The idea of working in a bank or an insurance company didn't appeal to me at all. I read about Kohl's plans in the paper and decided the German Chancellery in Bonn was the only appropriate place for a blonde to do a training programme.

So along with hundreds of others I sent off my application and, lo and behold, was shortlisted for an interview. A few weeks later, there I was sitting in front of a selection committee comprised exclusively of men in the German Chancellery in Bonn.

The five committee members eyed me. I eyed them back. They asked me for my personal details and then wanted to know why I was the right candidate for a training programme in the Chancellery and what I wanted to learn. I'd already learned to respond to questions I couldn't give a satisfactorily intelligent answer to with a counter-question: 'What awaits me here and what is the subject of the training programme?'

The selection committee members looked at each other at a loss. They had absolutely no idea themselves. Since Kohl had made this decision, everything had happened so quickly that the training programmes had not passed the planning phase. At the end of the day, we were all convinced that in our clueless state we were the perfect match and we decided to give it a go.

I was offered one of two training posts in the administrative service of the German Chancellery. I ended up spending just over three years at the government's headquarters in Bonn. I learned a lot there, and am still very grateful for this today. It was a wonderful time."

Michael said I was a laugh. On the side, he continued to answer incoming texts. It began to dawn on me that he probably found my monologue convenient (giving him the chance to answer his messages) rather than entertaining. I certainly wasn't getting his undivided attention.

All the talk had made me even hungrier than before, so we finally called the waiter. I ordered mini spring rolls and yakitori skewers with chicken as a starter and duck in plum sauce and rice as my main course.

GourmetSnob looked at me, his eyes wide in disbelief.

"Is that all for you? You're going to eat all that? I don't know any woman who can eat that much!"

Michael's metabolism was evidently less efficient than my own and he went without a starter, but he also chose the duck in plum sauce.

Unfortunately, I didn't like the man in the least and found his self-absorbed, emotionless manner repellent. It couldn't be easy having a relationship with a person like this. Sitting opposite me was another man with clearly narcissistic tendencies. I have to admit, though, the way he bad-mouthed fellow board members in his company did have a certain entertainment value.

He openly admitted that he earned pots of money and that he'd discovered a clever way of maximising results with minimum effort.

"You know, you don't have to work yourself to death just because you're a senior member of company. I'm happy to let others take over. I only do what I want to do, and just pretend I'm busy all day. As I am now – sitting here with you having a nice meal."

He winked at me conspiratorially and continued to comment on his life skills:

"I'm always travelling around visiting business partners. I have no idea what the point of it all is, but you know, time passes faster this way. I'd go mad if I had to spend all day in the office."

I smiled. Merlin had been absolutely right in his assessment. Michael definitely knew all the tricks. He was a very clever man, not to mention surprisingly candid in his descriptions of his professional life. His private life was a different matter, as I would learn later.

We chatted about our shared passion: food and wine. I had originally wanted to become a chef after I left school, and Michael told me he also loved cooking. His wine collection sounded impressive – my little wine cupboard was modest by comparison.

"You know, I'm friends with a number of very well-known restaurateurs. Good food is a matter of course for me."

I rolled my eyes inwardly.

Michael had been separated from his wife and three children for several years, but was still married. They weren't in a hurry to divorce, for the sake of the children, he explained. I didn't have a problem with that – as long as everything was settled and out in the open. When I asked him how long he'd been single, Michael started to stutter.

"Mmmm ... well ... actually ... I still have a girlfriend. Up on the coast in north Germany. I'm in the process of splitting up from her though. My cases are already packed, as it were. It's all over. The last two years were enough. I never really wanted a relationship with her in the first place. I just sort of slipped into it. She's 12 years younger than me, the age difference is just too much. She wants children. I've been there, done that. I already have three kids of my own."

At that moment, I'd like to have thwacked him across the head.

"You're still married, you have a girlfriend up in north Germany, and you write to other women? Was your bathwater too hot this morning?"

The candidate had well and truly screwed things up. There would most definitely be no follow-up date with

Michael. I advised him to sort out his private life and take a long, honest look at himself in his bathroom mirror. My lunch date was over. I got up and left.

GourmetSnob was evidently not put off by my abrupt departure. On the contrary, it seemed to arouse his hunting instinct. In the following weeks, he continued to send me WhatsApp messages and try to persuade me to meet him again. He 'love bombed' me, even sent me a marriage proposal and planned having a family with me. I found it all more than odd.

Naturally, he didn't change his personal situation and continued to spend the weekends with his younger girlfriend. It became increasingly clear to me that I really had met a man with a narcissistic personality.

I'd always been convinced that online dating was not for me, but until the start of my dating adventure, had never really asked myself why. I'd been instinctively sceptical about the kind of men out there in the online dating world. Gradually, I was beginning to understand why.

Eventually, Michael gave up.

I didn't hear from him for over a year. Then suddenly, out of the blue, he sent me a WhatsApp message asking me if I'd like to go out for dinner. His personal situation was still the same.

I didn't need his company. I sent him a smiley in response and deleted him from my address book forever.

5. Date: Don Quixote

Why, in heaven's name, had I decided to embark on this online dating lark? After almost every date, I spent hours under an oxygen tent, trying to recover from the ordeal.

But one question I kept asking myself was why millions of women do this apparently of their own free will and on a long-term basis? True, men have strange experiences with women too. As I haven't dated any women, though, I can only talk about my experiences with men.

On the other hand, I found it increasingly interesting to look at the psychological backgrounds of these men and examine internet dating in general. I resolved to continue until I had met my last dating candidate. Maybe I'd find my match after all.

Don Quixote (54 years old, star sign Virgo)

The next candidate cultivated an interesting linguistic style in his messages, and evidently he too had got wind of my blog and love of France. There was also an Anglo-American side to him. Mixing languages, he wrote:

"Bonjour Princess, incroyable, let's give the next step a try. Just an idea, but do you have time next week for a coffee, lunch or early dinner at five and a glass of Champagne? If so, when would be the best time?"

Finding dinner at 5 pm about as erotic as a parking meter, and never touching Champagne before 6, I proposed two possible dates for lunch.

"*Baroness* (authorities on nobility will have noticed a de-motion had already taken place), *no worris [sic]. Drop me a line! Is any day good, or do you have a préférence? 12.30, c'est trop tot? CU Philip."*

The photo Philip had sent me of a himself was of a *"tall, slender, well-toned man"*, as he described himself. Certainly elegant in appearance.

We agreed to meet in a little bistro. Beforehand, as always, I asked Merlin to take a look at the candidate's astrological data.

"A clever guy with very alert eyes. He has a Sun-Pluto conjunction. These people sometimes have divine aspi-rations. People who have Mercury in Leo tend to take things personally. You have to be careful. That can be a challenge for a cheeky Sagittarius like you.

Outwardly, he seems to be sensible and understand-ing, but he can be ruthless. He justifies his decisions with logical, calm arguments and is probably a very successful businessman. He definitely has managerial qualities, but unfortunately there are also some narcis-sistic traits."

Philip was the managing director of a large commercial cleaning services company which he had set up many years ago. If his lifestyle – as documented in his many profile photos – was anything to go by, he'd made a lot of money with this business.

"Once he's made a decision, he finds it hard to go back on it. He is very concerned about security and doesn't like unpleasant surprises. In fact, it wouldn't surprise me if he asked you for your medical records. He's impertinent, but pretends to be sensible. He's an adaptable egomaniac, but he's an easy-going kind of guy too. You could have a fun time."

I was very curious to meet the boss of the cleaning services company.

He was already waiting for me at the restaurant, and he greeted me with a certain gentility and reserve.

But can you believe where the man was sitting? On a chair facing the restaurant! Mon Dieu! He'd basically failed my test even before he'd opened his mouth.

Gentlemen, just to make proper protocol perfectly clear: the man lets the woman have the best seat in a restaurant, in other words, the one facing the room. The man, on the other hand, can look at a wall. After all, he should be concentrating on the most beautiful thing in the room, the woman sitting opposite him. Before this, he holds the door open for her and helps her out of her coat. On a first date, if he wants to be the perfect gentleman, he'll also pay the bill.

I stopped myself from commenting on his choice of seat, sat down on my chair and looked at the pockmarked yellow wall behind him.

The man opposite me was very pale and seemed a little jittery. Elegantly dressed, of slim build, with slightly dishevelled greying hair that flopped over his forehead. The unkempt hairstyle didn't really suit him. In all other respects, he was immaculately turned out, almost bureaucratically boring and a bit stuffy.

Philip had already ordered a bottle of water. We glanced briefly at the small menu and from the list of delicious-sounding pasta dishes, I chose spaghetti carbonara with extra parmesan. Philip raised his eyebrows and remarked pointedly:

"You eat carbohydrates? Astonishing. Most women usually avoid them like the plague."

"Carbohydrates are pretty high up on my agenda. I love pasta, and I love French fries too. I can't get enough of them!"

"Right … I'm more careful. I eat more salads and vegetables, but I guess you know what you're doing."

Philip raised his eyebrows in a slightly disapproving manner and eyed me critically. He was really something of a party pooper.

Generally, I think it's a commendable quality in a man if he watches his figure. Football-sized beer bellies simply aren't sexy. Enjoyment of good food is important to me though, and I don't choose what I eat according to calories and would certainly never dream of ruining my companion's meal. I'm a great fan of the saying 'Live and let live'.

Philip pushed himself further back on the bench, his back upright. I sprawled on my chair and like ET was desperate to phone home.

"Tell me something about yourself, Corinna. You didn't write much in your message. What do you do professionally? I didn't really understand what you wrote."

I looked at Philip with sad eyes and leaned my head sideways.

"Well, at the moment, things are going really badly. I need a man with money. The jobs have just dried up. I have to share my flat with a male student from Russia."

As was my intention, Philip's spirits sank and he looked at me with a slightly disgusted expression.

"You what? You live with a man? Is there something going on with him? That's a weird set-up."

I had to pinch myself to stifle my laughter and keep a straight face.

"Victor and I can't keep our hands off each other."

There was that inward eye-roll again. Philip still hadn't realised I was kidding – although, as it happened, I actually was temporarily sharing my flat with Victor.

A friend of mine had asked me to put him up for a while as he was having problems finding somewhere to live. I agreed without hesitation. It seemed incredible, but being a foreigner and a PhD student had evidently not been beneficial in his flat-hunting endeavours.

Between you and me, I'll admit, I'm really the inventor of Airbnb! Those guys just pinched the idea from me and were clever enough to turn it into a multi-trillion-dollar business. Incidentally, this is an excellent example of how business ideas repeatedly rejected by investors can ultimately turn into something really successful ... :-)

Victor and I had great fun together and we are still good friends today. I'll never forget the first time he turned up at my door.

It was a dark October evening and pouring with rain. The bell rang, and there stood my PhD student Victor. "Cooooonnny, here I am!" he boomed, dragging several suitcases and plastic bags into the house from the rain-drenched street, beaming at me.

After just two minutes, my hallway looked like it had been hit by a nuclear bomb. The plastic bags and cases left little pools of water all over the parquet floor and my two cats frolicked delightedly in the puddles.

This could be the start of an interesting experience, I thought. And indeed it was. Victor and I got on like a house on fire. We spent many an evening cooking, eating, drinking wine (him and me) and vodka (him), singing and dancing together. Late at night, we even came up with our own meditation exercises. Buddha would have been proud of us.

Once Victor had understood that a full fridge (which he had to provide in lieu of rent) consisted not only of vodka and beer, our flat-share arrangement turned out to be an enormous success. I didn't enter his room or bathroom once. I don't think I could have handled the chaos.

When it came to men, Victor also became a valuable adviser. His assessments almost always turned out to be accurate.

We also taught each other important things about our respective cultures. For example, I learned that a Russian man has to pay his partner lots of compliments during the day – otherwise he'll be welcomed with a plate over his head in the evening.

Since then, I've always kept sufficient supplies of plain white porcelain in my house, realising that somewhere I have Russian blood in me ...

After less than half an hour, I knew that with a man like Philip I'd need to replenish my supplies of porcelain every week. He was simply too dull and too joyless.

Thankfully, our food was served promptly and I twisted my spaghetti around my fork in record-breaking time. Pretending I had an urgent appointment to go to, I asked the kind waitress (who Philip had ticked off when he'd placed his order) for the bill.

This dullest of dates cost me 60 minutes of my life and €46.80. Would you believe it, the managing director had forgotten his wallet!

6. Date: Merman007

My next date was a formidable case in more ways than one.

First off, he had a belly the size of a basketball, not just a football.

However, beauty lies within, or so the saying goes, so I magnanimously resolved to overlook his physical proportions.

Secondly, the man was not a complete unknown in Germany and I was surprised that someone with his professional background dared to date women online. At that moment, I had no idea I was in for even more surprises, but one thing at a time.

Merman007 (49 years old, Aries, Taurus rising)

Nearly two metres tall and with his enormous belly, the man really couldn't be missed. He had short, dark brown curly hair, friendly green eyes, and very pale skin. In photos or interviews on TV, he always wore the same clothes: a dark suit with a white shirt, no tie. Or if he wanted to look more casual, he'd swap the suit trousers for a pair of beige jeans.

His writing style was rather odd, but I didn't dislike it. He pestered me until I gave him my phone number so that we could text.

"Good day, Frau B. It's a sunny day and I'm delighted to hook up with you on WhatsApp. I'm sending you holiday greetings and will be in touch again by phone in the next few days (after my holiday, next week)."

"Hello, Anton, Thanks for your message. Enjoy the rest of your holiday. Relax and have fun."

Anton was evidently not into cycling along beach promenades or swimming in the sea. He bombarded me with WhatsApp messages, unaware of the fact he was walking on a minefield. Not wanting to be a complete killjoy, I replied to the occasional message. Sometimes, he texted me up to 50 times a day. After only a few days, this just seemed really odd.

"This fine gentleman isn't always as sweet as he is on holiday. You're lucky, Frau B., he's putting up a good show. Some men don't bother with all the sweet talk and get straight to the point."

If I didn't answer his messages immediately, it wasn't without consequences. I'd already told him I hated constant texting.

"If WhatsApp is the reason for disruptions in our communication flow, we can switch back to the dating site. Frau Busch, you're definitely something special. A man has to be on his guard with you though. I look forward to what lies ahead."

The last but one sentence confirmed a niggling fear I'd had for a while.

"Why should a man be on his guard with me?"

"Control."

The phrase 'not quite right in the head' sprang to mind. A rather crude description of a serious, possibly pathological condition, true, but I'd obviously picked yet another man with narcissistic tendencies.

I was less than enthusiastic about meeting the portly Merman, but Merlin was bowled over by the candidate's horoscope.

"He really does have an interesting horoscope. A late Aries, early Taurus. He's really torn, because he's constantly on the run. He's a very intelligent man, interested in higher values and willing to die like a crusader for an ideology. He might also be close to the Church."

Indeed, Anton had told me he'd been a teacher of religion at a high school years previously, before setting up his own business.

"The man has warrior-like skills, but at the same time he's willing to make sacrifices and is by nature an inquisitive person. He's prepared to give his all, but he expects the same from others. I'm afraid he's in a completely different orbit than you. But make an effort to get to know him personally."

Anton was very busy (or at least pretended to be) so it was a while before we were actually able to arrange a lunch date. He kept promising to suggest a time, but then never did. Instead, he continued to write one text message after the next.

"You make me look at my phone around twenty times a day."

"Why the devil do you do that?"

"Because somehow I like you and your style. There's nothing superficial about you. You're neither easy, nor are you always strong. But please leave the devil out of it. I don't like that kind of talk."

"You don't know me, Anton, you don't know what's under the surface! But I'd be happy to meet you for lunch. I always love a good meal. Otherwise I'm going to have to put an end to all this writing. Four weeks of texting are enough for me."

"I like your directness, Frau Busch. I like the way you speak your mind. Okay, so would you be free next Thursday lunchtime?"

"Yes, I can arrange that."

"Great. I'll neither work nor will I allow myself to fall ill. The end of the world will be postponed, the train will run, my armour will be polished. I'll apply for my visa, wrestle with dragons and princes at the city walls, put off making my speech on the state of the nation, and I'll be prepared for all eventualities".

"Great, I'll be there at about 1 pm."

"But only if it's convenient, Frau Busch."

"Yes, Anton, it is. I'm already looking forward to my schnitzel. They're especially crispy in this restaurant."

I was actually expecting Anton to cancel at the last minute but he turned up at the restaurant at one on the dot.

The man was at least 40 kilos overweight and probably as a consequence slightly short-winded. It was a hot summer day and little beads of sweat gathered on his forehead. Every so often, he dabbed them away with a checked handkerchief. I imagined the white shirt under his dark suit jacket to be drenched.

We looked for a quiet corner on the large, shady restaurant terrace and ordered an apple spritz to quench our thirst. I watched Merman as he studied the menu.

Despite his corpulence, this friendly-looking man reminded me of an insecure little boy. Perhaps this insecurity was one of the reasons for his obesity.

Anton seemed to read my thoughts.

"I know, Frau Busch, I know, I really must eat more salad and vegetables and do something about my weight. I'll start straight away and just order a salad with grilled turkey breast."

"Anton, eat whatever you want! You must feel comfortable in your own body, and it's your health. I'm going to have schnitzel with sautéed potatoes."

"That's mean! You're as thin as a pencil and you get away with eating food like that!"

"It must be my father's genes. He used to eat like a horse but was always as super thin. Of course I do make sure I eat a healthy diet though. I don't eat schnitzel every day. But when the fancy takes me, I love to tuck into a crisp, breadcrumb-coated escalope of veal."

Anton laughed.

"Frau Busch, you and your comments! That's what I like about you. You get straight to the point. I do feel overweight though. All the work stress and business dinners I have to attend – it's hard eating in moderation. I also stopped smoking a year ago. That made me put on weight."

When Anton spoke, he did so in a quiet, deliberate manner. His voice reminded me of that of a pastor. We chatted about our work, and I enjoyed listening to him, the business man, philosophise about his view of the world and society.

We got involved in a lengthy discussion about sustainable economic policy, and the time just flew by. This was without doubt an intelligent and charismatic man, yet something inside me warned me about Anton. He kept stressing the fact that he was a well-known person in Germany, mentioning comments he'd made and where he'd been quoted in the media. Something else that irritated me was how often he spoke about his wife. In one of his many text messages, he had assured me he was divorced.

"You often mention your wife, Anton. It's good you still

get on after your divorce. I always find it sad when couples who were once in love stop speaking to each other after they separate."

"Mmmm ...yes ..., Frau Busch. You've mentioned an important subject. This is my second marriage. Now don't get angry with me, I didn't lie to you because I really am divorced, but only from my first wife. You wouldn't have met me otherwise. My second wife and I have separated but it's just not official yet."

"What do you mean 'not official yet'? Does your wife know you're separated or would she be surprised to hear it? Nobody apart from you knows, am I right, Anton?"

"Of course I've talked to my wife about it. Why are you confronting me like this? We're having such a nice lunch together. I'm really taken with you. It's like I've been struck by lightning."

"That's not the point. You've deceived me, and deliberately so. I wouldn't have met you if I'd known you were married."

Why don't men (and women, too) make the effort to finish relationships before throwing themselves head first into the next?

"I have to sort myself out. If I couldn't imagine you being capable of turning my life upside down, Frau Busch,

I wouldn't be sitting here now. There are a lot of needs my wife can't satisfy. I believe you could."

I refrained from making any more remarks about satisfying his needs, thanked him for the invitation to lunch and made a quick exit. As far as I was concerned, that was the end of the matter.

For Anton, however, it was far from over. He text-bombed me, professing his love for me and fantasising about the S&M practices he had (allegedly) not yet tried out. He sent me pictures of himself inserting hot needles through his nipples (thank goodness I couldn't tell whether they really were his nipples) and claimed he wanted to be my bedside rug, my slave.

Irrespective of whether or not anyone can warm to such practices, I found it bizarre that a man could bombard a woman with messages like this after a single meeting. He was not in the least bit sensitive. I became convinced Anton led a kind of double life and that in all likelihood I was not his only online date. He travelled extensively and had plenty of opportunities to keep at least one lady in every port.

I politely asked him to stop sending me any more contact requests and texts – but to no avail. Eventually – although it seemed silly – I had to block him. He left me no other choice. Nothing about Anton was, or appeared to be light. Everything was heavy – outwardly and inwardly and in our communication with each other.

Even now, as I write these lines some time later, I realise how much energy this man tried to deprive me of. Fortunately, it only remained an attempt. I'm a cheerful soul and not easily thrown off track.

As far as I know, Anton is still married and lives with his second wife.

7. Date: freshandgentle

After the portly Merman, Candidate No. 7 promised to offer at least physically some appealing qualities. Barely half my age, his messages abounded with that natural, flirtatious charm only southern Europeans can get away with. He purred like a tom cat.

freshandgentle (24 years old, Libra, Libra rising)

"Such a pretty, nice-looking woman. And if I may say so, such a lovely figure."

"Thank you, Tonio, that's a nice compliment."

"I'd really like to meet you. Do you always dress so elegantly? You look fantastic in your pictures."

"Another compliment! Thank you! No, at home I like pottering around in my pyjamas."

"Do you wear high heels a lot? Fortunately, I'm tall so you could wear heels all the time. I really like your style with your heels. It's really sexy."

As if the man didn't have more serious things to worry about! My bunions bulged even bigger at the thought of being permanently squeezed into pumps.

Tonio was Spanish by birth and had just started his first job after graduating from university with a degree in marketing. Almost two metres tall, numerous photos showed off his well-toned, firm and sexy body. His skin was smooth and bronzed, his black hair wavy.

Again I wondered what might drive such a young man into the no-longer-quite-so-wrinkle-free arms of a woman twice his age.

Maybe Merlin could shed some light on the matter. He studied the horoscope and a picture of Tonio and, at first, didn't utter a word.

"Well, well, well … now this really is a handsome man. And he's the boss. He's very self-centred. It's all me, me, me and me again."

I looked at Merlin as he shook his head slowly.

"His partners either leave voluntarily or he sends them packing, along the lines of 'You're fired'. What resonates with you is the fact that he's a Libra with Libra rising, you are very responsive to Libra qualities such as creativity and aesthetics."

I had to agree with Merlin. If a man has a feel for aesthetics, in my books, that certainly does no harm.

"Your candidate has Venus in Sagittarius, so we could assume he's interesting. He's certainly very clever and he also has a strong character. Even when he was a kid, he'd tell his mother 'Mum, the sun always shines on me'. He's not aware that others need the sun too."

Was I only ever going to meet narcissistic men who only wanted to have some fun and satisfy their own ego? I seriously considered taking an extended holiday and abandoning my dating experiment there and then.

But what if Candidate 12 was the man of my dreams? What did Nietzsche say again ... ? "The happy ones are curious." So I put on a brave face.

Tonio was keen, and he contacted me every day.

"Hello, lovely lady, shall we have a meal or a drink together next week? Do you have time?

"Hi Tonio, that would be nice. How about Wednesday around noon?"

"No problem. I'll take a longer lunch break. Looking forward to it. It's not every day you meet such a lovely, attractive woman. Who knows what might come of it!"

The man seemed to have a fundamentally optimistic outlook which I found appealing.

On the day of our meeting, he sent me a text at the crack of dawn.

"Are you looking forward to our meeting? Are you curious? I'll have to dress up today."

This time, I wanted to be absolutely certain my date was single and I asked him once again to confirm this in writing. I was feeling generous and refrained from requesting notarised certification.

"Are you really single?"

It didn't take long for him to confirm this.

"Yes, definitely. I look more or less like I do in my photos, only my hair is shorter and today I'm wearing jeans, a shirt and a green jacket."

Green, the colour of hope.

After every winter, new life springs forth again. Tender green shoots appear, trees burst into leaf. Would Tonio be the end of my personal winter, my time as a single woman? Could there be hope for an explosion of nature? Would I enjoy a second spring with Tonio?

When the young man approached me in the restaurant, I knew within seconds that it wasn't yet time to put my winter coat back into the wardrobe. Opposite me stood a Spanish puppy, so cute you wanted to cuddle him.

"Hello, lovely lady, I'm Tonio."

"Silky coat, bright shiny eyes and slender, nice-shaped legs" was obviously looking for a new home. His mother had sent him out to get some fresh air, he had told me. She believed that at 24, he was old enough to look after himself and live in his own apartment. Plus he earned more than she did.

"Your mother was absolutely right Tonio, and to make things absolutely clear, my dear, you're too old for me."

Tonio, who was about to drink from a rather beautiful crystal glass, flinched, choked on the water and had a violent coughing fit. Gesticulating wildly, the hot-blooded Spaniard also managed to knock over his glass of wine.

"I'm what? I'm too old for you? I'm 23 years younger than you!"

His brown eyes no longer looked beguiling, they were angry. I couldn't help thinking of football coach Giovanni Trapattoni's legendary 1998 press conference. *How dare I?* Toni continued to cough and splutter and I fanned air at him with my napkin.

"I'm not interested in adopting adults and I don't want to be your new mother or housekeeper. Let's just have a nice meal and a chat."

It took Tonio a while to calm down. Obviously accustomed to the sun shining on him all the time, he was having trouble coping with rejection, and yet I found him to be a very likeable man.

After a while, he relaxed and we talked about a passion we both shared: travelling the world. We counted off the countries we'd both visited and showed each other photos on our phones, so it turned out to be an entertaining lunch after all. To my surprise, Tonio insisted on paying, and I agreed.

For a while, he continued to send me occasional messages, filling me in on his dating experiences with other women. Eventually he found a girlfriend, a stewardess who served him an especially aromatic coffee on a flight to Spain.

8. Date: Luxurysecondhand 007

What to make of a man with a profile name like this?

Luxurysecondhand 007 (49 years old, Aries, Leo rising)

007, James Bond's famous code number, appeared frequently in men's profile names. What were they trying to tell you? Were they on a secret mission (because they were still married or in a relationship)? Were they especially suave and handsome? Afraid of deep feelings and more of a passing fancy?

Why 'luxury' second hand? Was he a multimillionaire? Rich and divorced? Had he outlived a wife and inherited her fortune? All kinds of ideas went through my head.

Thomas' profile picture showed a friendly-looking man, bald, black glasses, black polo-necked jumper. The picture only showed him down to his middle and unfortunately the black jumper made it impossible to guess what was hidden below. His face was a normal oval shape, but that didn't mean anything. I'd come to realise that a football-sized belly could lurk beneath any face.

Merlin was laid up with the flu, so this time, I had to prepare for my date without any astrological support. I was generally optimistic about his star sign, Aries. In my experience, two fire signs were usually a good match, but his message to me prompted slightly mixed feelings.

Dear Ms Corinna,

I would like to be considered as an applicant for the vacancy in your life.

It was with great interest that I read your description, and your photos made a positive initial impression on me.

My CV covers a number of areas I would like to outline as follows:

I am a young-at-heart 49-year-old, male and currently 1.84 m tall. I used to be a natural blond, now I wear a wide parting.

To be able to see my surroundings and you in sharp focus, I wear finely tuned lenses framed by a composite material made of horn (and I don't know what else) on my nose. The enclosed picture will give you a first impression (in case you haven't already seen it).

I currently weigh 89 kg, most of this being muscles (obviously ...) ;-).

To keep this dream body in shape, I frequently visit a nearby gym to strengthen and tone my muscles. By 'nearby' I mean a town near the beautiful city of Heidelberg, where I have a one-room residence.

Professionally, I have travelled extensively all over Germany for some time now with no end in sight. I leave home on Sundays, and return again on Thursdays. Nights are usually spent in hotels.

What do I do? I'm a successful SAP consultant for a retail trading group. If SAP consultant means anything to you, that's great! If not, it doesn't matter either. If you have any questions about my position, I would be happy to tell you in person.

There are obviously other aspects to my life. Let's start with the positive ones: I have two sons.

The negative one: they don't live with me. They live with

their mother and we are currently in the middle of a bitter
divorce battle. The three of them don't live in Heidelberg, but
in the family home not far from Heidelberg. I'll spare you the
details, but again, feel free to take up my offer of discussing
everything when we meet.

Apart from work and all life's other inconveniences, I relax
by playing sport, visiting friends (friends are very important!),
going to the cinema, reading or just lounging in front the TV.
Every now and then I enjoy a good meal too.

In the summer I like going out on my mountain bike. For me,
this is a form of relaxation but also a lot of fun!

If you are impressed by my letter of application, dear Ms.
Corinna, then I would be very happy to meet you.

Mondays to Wednesday are the most convenient days for me.
I look forward to a positive response.
Best wishes,
Thomas

I had trouble finding any sign of the 'luxury' mentioned in
his profile name, but the second-hand aspect was crystal
clear. I was truly grateful to the man for sparing me the
details of his ongoing divorce.

He still seemed somewhat ravaged by the Battle of
Somewhere-Close-to-Heidelberg. Even though I trained
as a mediator after studying law, I was by no means eager
to enter the battlefield as a negotiator. I do enough of that
in my professional life.

On the other hand, of all my dating candidates, Thomas
had written by far the longest message, and that, I thought,
deserved a reward.

Dear Mr Thomas,

Thank you very much for your enthusiastic letter of application!

It is a pleasure for me to inform you that you have made it into the next round. You have been shortlisted for a coffee and an introductory meeting.

Please feel free to contact me via text to arrange an appointment.

"Oh goodness, I can't believe I actually wrote all that, or that you have read it. Do you have time tomorrow for a coffee? That would be really nice. Feel free to suggest a place where we could meet. Best wishes, Thomas."

We agreed to meet at a small café two days later. I arrived ten minutes before the agreed time and managed to grab the last free table in the sun. I ordered a cappuccino and waited.

And waited ... and waited.

A well-known sportsman was sitting at a table in the far corner of the restaurant terrace. To my surprise, he chain-smoked. He was engrossed in his newspaper, his brow was deeply furrowed. Perhaps my new prescription sunglasses exaggerated my visual acuity but everything seemed big, sharp and close.

While I was sitting there waiting for Thomas with the sportsman nearby, a number of episodes I'd experienced with celebrity clients over the last 20 years went through my head.

For example, I had one famous actor client who travelled all over the world, only returning home to change his clothes. A housekeeper looked after his apartment and two cats. The actor had a huge 250-square-metre apartment with multiple rooms spread over three floors.

Returning from one of his trips one day, I picked him up from the airport and drove him to his apartment. His housekeeper opened the door to us. We were shocked to see the woman's entire right arm was bandaged up. My client dropped his bags and hugged his fairy godmother.

"Anna, what happened?"

"Moritz bit me and scratched me all over."

My client and I looked at each other dismayed. Max and Moritz were quite old and usually very placid cats. We couldn't believe Moritz's behaviour at all. My client told his housekeeper to take a few days off to recover. She grabbed her bag and disappeared out of the apartment.

The actor was a kind-hearted person and plagued with guilt about what had happened. His cat had bitten the poor woman! He racked his brains about what to do, and then decided to buy her a gift and take it round to her home. No sooner said than done.

I accompanied him to his housekeeper's apartment. The good fairy opened the door and didn't seem particularly pleased to see the actor. Hesitantly, she let us in, inviting us to take a seat in the living room while she called for her daughter.

I looked around the room. Somehow, some of the objects there looked familiar. I nudged my client and pointed to a chest of drawers.

"Haven't you got a sculpture like that at home?"

My client froze. After a few seconds, he went over to the sculpture, picked it up, and looked closely at the bottom.

"I don't believe it! It's my sculpture! There's a dedication written to me underneath."

"Look at that picture over there! Didn't your mother give that to you for your birthday? Those tumblers on the table look familiar too!"

I stood up and opened the glass cabinet. Most of the contents belonged to my client.

The good fairy was in reality a witch. Over a period of time, she had removed objects worth over €40,000 from my client's apartment and taken them to her own home.

My client was shocked to the core. He had trusted the woman blindly, but what shook him perhaps most was that he hadn't even noticed his belongings were missing. He lived in such abundance that one painting or set of glasses less made no difference to him.

Meanwhile, back on the café terrace, I'd finished my cappuccino, and there was still no sign of Thomas. I wrote him a text asking whether he still planned to grace me with his presence. I never heard from him again.

9. Date: Specialmodel66

My next dating candidate turned out to be a complicated heavyweight. In his first message to me, the subject line read 'Special model & TOP manager' and contained a link to his profile in a professional networking site. I found this so bizarre I decided to add him to my list of 12 finalists. I wanted to take a personal look at this gentleman.

Specialmodel66 (49 years old, Sagittarius, Libra rising)

His profile photo on the dating site showed only a blurred image down to his chest. Beneath that I suspected a belly worthy of a twin pregnancy.

Merlin took a brief look at my dating candidate's astrological profile.

"The man moves between light and shadow. He's an outspoken, tough sort of guy, totally success-oriented. The ruler of his House of Partnership is Mars and Mars is his ruling planet, nobody is as good as him and nobody can match his standards. He's quick to find fault in people, and probably has problems in his relationships because he's so dominant. The next egomaniac. He has a soft side, but he's very scared of anyone noticing it. Being provocative is his way of protecting himself from being hurt."

Reiner wrote me only a few, inconsequential lines and asked me to give him my mobile number "so that it would be easier to arrange a date", he explained pragmatically. By this point, I was completely unfazable and could hardly wait for his texts.

"Dear Corinna, thank you for your trust. I look forward to meeting you."

"Hello Reiner, why is your picture on the dating site so blurred? Your text message profile picture only shows a villa, presumably somewhere in Tuscany."

"I only want to show pictures of myself to women I like."

"Interesting. Does that mean I need a tranquiliser before I get to see your face?"

This reply was apparently too bold for Mr TOP Manager.

"No, there's nothing wrong with my looks, all's fine. I'm not so sure about yours yet."

How about that for a compliment!

"Well, there are two pictures of me on my dating profile."

"Can I ask you where you live? Please send me two photos of yourself, a full-body shot and a photo of your profile."

The man obviously pursued a very distinct online shopping strategy. Given that my declared goal was to meet him in person, I did a ten-minute sun salutation, took a deep breath and returned, full of positive energy, to my keyboard. I vowed to remain as sweet as sugar, no matter how insulting my online dating partner became.

"I live in the Rhineland and in Munich. I'm happy to show you more pictures when we meet for launch."

I noticed my typo and corrected myself in my next message. His reply was prompt:

"Okay, maybe you can't help making stupid spelling mistakes. Whatever. I'll be in Cologne next week and could fit in a meeting then, but only in the evening. I have meetings all day."

The thought of having to spend my precious free time with this Prince Charming gave me nervous convulsions. My evenings are really sacred to me.

I love to cook, but sometimes cooking for one is too much of an effort. If I have no appointments or other commitments, I like to eat out early at a restaurant (since I usually miss lunch). I mull over the day, enjoy some good food and people-watch. Occasionally, I'll listen in to conversations at neighbouring tables and write short stories about them (the attentive reader will have already recognised one such eavesdropping session earlier in this book).

I suggested dinner at one of Cologne's most expensive restaurants and decided that on this evening, I would leave my purse at home. To my astonishment, the man accepted without further discussion.

On the day of our agreed meeting, Reiner sent me a text in the morning confirming our dinner date. It read a little like a customer confirming a hostess service. I'd made a point of having my body measurements checked so that, if required, I could give him my current cup size (which varies according to weight), leg length and waist circumference, but no further data was requested in advance.

My subconscious was probably doing its best to resist a meeting with 'Mr TOP Manager'. Flustered, I arrived at the restaurant ten minutes late and asked after a reservation for Reiner. It was only then that I realised my date had texted to say he would be half an hour late himself. I sat down on seat facing the restaurant and waited.

Enjoy life, we only live once.

It's important to make someone happy, and it's important to start with yourself.

A few days before, I'd come across my old autograph book again and was surprised to read some of the sayings which had been immortalised on its pages. The red cover with its small white dots and cute embroidered duck was rather worn, but the individual pages were in good condition. The book was still in my handbag, so I took it out and leafed through it as I waited.

If bad boys get your hormones rocking, stay at home and darn your stockings.

Maybe I should have followed my old school friend Heike's advice – although I don't darn stockings and can't imagine a more tedious task. The only thing that's worse than the dreariness of darning stockings is waiting over half an hour for a date.

Forty-five minutes after the agreed time, a tsunami hit me with full force. Plonking himself heavily onto a wooden chair opposite me, the fragile legs promptly gave way beneath the 120-kg manager who only just stopped himself from hitting the floor by grabbing hold of an unsuspecting waiter. The latter, in turn, latched on to a heavily laden cheese trolley which wobbled and toppled over, catapulting its entire contents across the restaurant's lovely black-and-white tiled floor and all over my manager's right trouser leg. Quite the entrance!

I'm no authority on cheese and can't say which of the finest French *fromages* was to blame, but a pungent smell filled the air, and the place was a mess.

Thanks to this film-like scene the evening, for me, had got off to a priceless start.

Red in the face, my date manoeuvred himself onto a hastily proffered tubular steel chair, and officiously ordered a glass of red wine. He then insisted on summoning the restaurant manager to complain about the "goddamned chairs". He could have broken his neck, he claimed, and would be consulting his lawyer about compensation – including for his designer suit, which now stank of cheese.

Then he looked at me.

"Why are you on a dating site? You look respectable enough to me. I read that you even studied law."

I bent across the table towards him (not too close because of the unpleasant odour) and spoke slowly and quietly:

"I'm writing a book about my dating experiences with men like you. I've already sold the film rights. And the camera installed back there in the corner has just recorded this little scene. I think you might be part of the trailer. That was a truly unique performance. The producers will be delighted."

The manager's eyes narrowed.

"You're joking, right? I know you're a media chick, but you can't be serious!"

"I made it up about the camera, but I really am writing a book."

"You're totally mad. I'm warning you. If I ever read anything about myself in your book, you've had it. My lawyers will finish you off."

I stood up again and left.

The next day I received a contact request on a professional networking platform from another senior manager. Reiner was one of his contacts. Was it a coincidence that an acquaintance of Reiner was contacting me a day after our date? Did he want to scan my professional profile page (on behalf of the dating candidate)? Reiner seemed genuinely alarmed. His profile on the dating site had been deleted.

I still wonder which actor I would cast in the role of Reiner if my book was ever filmed. Maybe I could even invite Mr TOP Manager to audition for the part.

10. Date: BuddyLove

By this point, I was on tablets. Vitamin B12. A lavender-scented pillow and lavender sachets stuffed inside my duvet helped calm my nerves and relax me at night. These and other purely natural remedies induced a coma-like sleep that I was greatly in need of.

Thanks to the cheese incident, I was once again on the verge of abandoning my dating experiment. But three pieces of paper still lay on the floor in front of me, and as inventor Thomas Alva Edison once said: "Our greatest weakness lies in giving up and the most certain way to succeed is always to try just one more time."

So taking a long, deep breath, I pulled out my next candidate.

BuddyLove (54 years old, Taurus, Capricorn rising)

The pictures were of a 1.75-metre-tall man with dark, slightly wavy, mid-length hair who wore maritime-style clothing. White or beige trousers were alternated with red or pink polo shirts. His face was tanned, his body trim and athletic. He told me he was a university lecturer.

As I read his message, I wondered what faculty he might belong to.

"Hello Conny, I'm Sven. I have no idea why, but first of all I thought you were called Cora. For some reason, Cora automatically made me think of porn. I have no idea why. But just for the record, this is not the reason why I'm writing to you, I'm writing because of your inspiring profile. I really can't explain

why your name made me think of porn, because that's really not my thing at all. The porn scene, I mean. I'm certainly someone who likes to enjoy himself, but not with the canned sort of entertainment. When it comes to eating, that can be a different matter, depending on the situation.

You're talented (did he mean that with regard to porn?), *I can already tell. I suspect you're a provocative and intelligent woman. Why don't you describe your day to me so far? Tell me what you're doing right now, what you did six hours ago and what you'll be doing in six hours' time* (I won't go into the meaning of the number six at this point). *Then tell me on a scale of 0* (shitty) *to 10* (orgasmic) *how much you enjoy doing these things.*

My day has been as follows: I woke up and then went back to bed again (6). Then I sat down at my computer and wondered about all the things I'd have to do to win over the lady in the two photos I'd just looked at (10). Now I'm finishing off an appraisal for a student (3), but other aspects of my job (which ones?) *are worth a 9, close to orgasmic. My students probably think I've lost it sometimes* (this did cross my mind)."

Just as I was wondering which university had been lucky enough to land BuddyLove, the next message arrived.

"*My heart is beating faster ... my blood pressure is rising ... Questions are emerging out of my foggy brain ... I want to ... Until just now I was only looking ... now it's time to take the next step ... throw oil on the fire ... or slow myself down ... I'm really emotional right now ... I'm so preoccupied with you I'm going to have to take a cold shower ... How annoying that you live so far away ... I need to take another cold shower ...*

I'm going to run out of water because of you ... You fasci-
nate me ... your skin ... your smell ... I would worship your
perfectly formed female curves if my hands were allowed to
touch them ... Okay, I've just had a glass of red wine and am
getting talkative. But I'm not a weirdo or a stalker. When
shall we meet?"

Did I miss something? Is there such a thing as digital
smell detection?

The man had never met me but was fascinated by my
smell?

I became seriously concerned about his students. Suddenly, I understood where his dating nickname 'Buddy-
Love' came from. In the American film *The Nutty Professor*,
Jerry Lewis, playing a rather mousy professor, swallows
a chemical potion that turns him into the attractive, but
arrogant, macho Buddy Love.

I spontaneously had the idea of evacuating all ten dates
to a desert island together, but then decided I'd wait until
I'd met all 12 men on list.

Merlin was unexpectedly invited to attend a conference,
so once again, I had to prepare for my date without his
astrological guidance. Taurus and Sagittarius are not always considered an ideal match. With a Sagittarius like
me, a Taurus may find himself on an expedition in the
Kalahari Desert faster than he'd like – though he'd probably rather sit home admiring his garden.

Apart from this, Mr. Weirdo, as he called himself, hadn't
exactly won me over with his prose. But maybe Sven was

really a good guy? I decided to give him a chance offline. This seemed to both relieve and delight him.

"I'm glad I haven't put you off. My enthusiasm sometimes gets the better of me – a woman has to be able to handle that, and emotions are the spice of life."

We arranged to meet in an English café for afternoon tea. On the day of our meeting, Sven sent me the following message at 10.12 am:

"Good morning, Conny, how are you? Looking forward to meeting you later."

"Good morning, Sven, thanks, I'm fine. I'll be at the café at the agreed time."

At 10.37 am, the next message arrived:

"Our date is still on?"

"Hello Sven, as far as I'm concerned, nothing has changed in the last 20 minutes."

"Great, Conny. Glad to hear it."

At 12.46 pm there was another message:

"Hello Conny, I'd like to cancel our date. I've had another think and have decided we live too far apart. Yours, Sven."

I told him I understood his decision, thanked him for the message and wished him all the best.

At 1.50 pm, another message arrived from BuddyLove:

"Can I change my mind again? I'd like to meet you after all. Today's a good day, and it's not complicated or difficult for me to get to you. And I've made time especially."

Perhaps I should arrange for that desert island evacuation after all.

2 pm. The next message from BuddyLove:

"Shall we meet outside the café, or how will I recognise you? Will you have a copy of The Times on the table?"

"I'll be singing loudly, Sven. I won't wait outside the café, I'll just go in and sit down."

"What? You'll sing? Oh no, please don't! It'll attract attention."

2.20 pm, message from BuddyLove:

"Conny, is it possible to park outside the café?"
   "The café doesn't have its own car park but there are enough spaces on the street."

2.45 pm, message from BuddyLove:

"Hello Conny, I've just heard there's a long tailback on the road. I'm afraid I'm going to have to cancel our meeting after all."

Using the time I now had on my hands, I started my research into remote, uninhabited islands.

11. Date: doublevision

I looked at the two remaining pieces of paper on the wooden floor of my office and played 'eeny meeny miny moe'. My index finger ended on the left-hand piece of paper.

Feeling rather weary, I stared at the floor for several minutes but still couldn't bring myself to pick up the note. Just to be sure, I tried 'O-U-T spells out goes he', ending again on the left-hand note. I resigned myself to my fate.

doublevision (51 years old, Capricorn, Aquarius rising)

The photo was of a very attractive man, born in Argentina but brought up in Germany. Short, slightly wavy black hair, green eyes, a pleasingly normal, athletic figure, 1.88 metres tall. He had set up several wholesale wine businesses and regularly travelled all over the world. An internationally successful entrepreneur. Why did he want to hook up with women online though? After everything I'd experienced so far, I was curious.

Astrologer Merlin was rather taken with my penultimate candidate.

"He's a charismatic and communicative man, and also very intelligent and sharp. An independent type, but one who does his best to be loyal and devoted to his family. I could imagine him leading two lives and think he might enjoy the occasional adventure. Are you sure he's single?"

This was a question I couldn't answer. On his profile page, Tito, as he was called, replied to the question 'Do you want a new relationship?' with a 'maybe'. By this time, I had come to realise that men often dreamed of quite different lifestyles to the ones they actually led.

"The man is very dynamic and any obstacles that stand in his way are immediately removed. He's like an insistent salesman. If you throw him out the front door, he'll come back through the back door five minutes later. If his company ship crashes into the harbour wall, he'll continue full throttle over a hill into the next ocean. I'm interested to see how your meeting with him goes."

Tito's messages were a mix of German, Spanish and English, and they were gratifyingly short.

"Hey Conny, how are you doing? Ich bin not a big writer, let's have a nice glass of Wein together soon und etwas essen. I'm not a fancy guy, I don't need any Sterne, just good food, nice company. What do you think? Muchos besos Tito."

After BuddyLove, this was an uncomplicated man of action. There was something refreshing about it. I was in the middle of a new project and travelling a lot, basically only coming home for a change of clothes.

"Hi Tito, a glass of wine would be nice. I'm away a lot for work at the moment. How's your schedule?"

"Hi Conny, I'm flying to Buenos Aires for six days. And you?"

"Lucky you! I'm flying to Los Angeles for five days tomorrow."

"Lucky you! Okay. C u after you and I return, okay? Muchos besos."

"Okay."

Ten days later, Tito sent me a text message.

"Hi Conny, sorry, I stayed in Buenos Aires longer than planned. How about a spontaneous drink this evening?"

"Sorry, I'm still in Zurich. How about next Wednesday or Thursday?"

"I'll be in Vienna. Won't get back until late. Friday?"

"That's when I fly to London. The week after, Tuesday?"

"Ah dammit, I have to go to Cape Town then, but only for three days. Saturday night?"

"I'll be in Prague. Back Sunday. Monday evening?"

"Bank dinner with business partners in Zurich."

This went on for almost four weeks and we were both amused by our pseudo-cosmopolitan lifestyles. It was like there was a jinx on us. There wasn't a single day when we were both in the same country at the same time. Having a relationship with someone like Tito would probably have an excellent chance of lasting a lifetime, because you'd only get to see each other five times a year – at the very most.

Eventually, we found an evening when we were both in the same country and had no appointments. On his way to the Italian bistro where we'd arranged to meet, Tito texted me at one-minute intervals, telling me which street corner his taxi had just passed. Being a passionate wine drinker, he said he always took a taxi to evening appointments. He suggested that whoever arrived last at the restaurant should pay the bill. Since I was not in a taxi but behind the wheel of my own car, I couldn't answer him. I only saw his messages pop up on the display of my phone, which I was using to navigate me to the restaurant.

When I arrived, Tito was already sitting on a seat facing the restaurant. He beamed at me. I inclined my head and eyed him. My simulated strictness worked. Tito immediately jumped up from his seat and greeted me with a hug.

"Hello Conny, I have two good pieces of news for you. First, you can have my seat so that you can see everything and everyone in the restaurant, and second, I will naturally foot the bill. That was a joke just now. If I ever ask you to pay when we eat out together, call the men in white coats straight away! There'll be something not quite right with me. I'm old school."

I believed him. Sitting opposite me was my first dating candidate who actually looked better offline than online. A South American oozing charm and charisma, with straight, pearly-white teeth. His dark grey suit fit perfectly while still looking casual. The top three buttons on his close-fitting lilac-coloured shirt had taken the evening off. The clothes, shoes, wristwatch were all undoubtedly expensive designer items, yet he didn't look overdressed or pretentious, merely classy and elegant. Despite his obvious wealth, he seemed down-to-earth, but he was also well aware of the impression he made.

Tito pulled the table out a little so that I could sit on the bench, then pushed it back into place and sat down on a wooden chair. We studied the surprisingly extensive menu in silence, both choosing the same starter and main course.

"Well, darling, that's a good sign. We seem to have the same taste."

He had a deep voice and spoke with a soft South American accent that heighted his seductive appeal. I could imagine it making him extremely successful with the ladies. The whole package was simply too good to be true. He was attractive, courteous, successful, wealthy and had homes in several countries.

I could literally smell a wife and children and decided to come straight to the point:

"Let's be direct and open with each other. If you're single, then I have two kids I never knew existed."

Tito set his glass of red wine slowly down on the dark brown wooden table, crossed his arms in front of his chest and looked at me with a slight smirk. He remained silent for a few seconds, his eyes twinkling.

"You're very smart and beautiful, mi amor, and it's not easy for a man to fool you. Yes, you're right, I'm married and have five children, three sons and two daughters."

He took his cell phone from the inside pocket of his jacket and showed me a photo of his family. It was of a good-looking woman with dark blonde hair and five incredibly beautiful children. The picture could have been an advert for designer clothing. They all looked like something straight out of a fashion magazine.

"Mi amor, that's how we men are. I still respect my wife and she's a great mother, but there are some things I miss. When we got married, we were young. She looked after the kids and I set up several businesses. When I think about myself today, I regret the fact, for example, that I can't discuss business matters with my wife. She's just not interested. She's not business-minded. Now that I'm older, I like independent, tough, but also sensual women."

"If that's how it is, why don't you talk to your wife?"

"There isn't anything to talk about. I can't leave my family. You don't do that in my clan."

"Do you think that's fair to the women you flirt with through online dating?"

"Come on, Conny, we all like a little variety every so often. Life is serious enough as it is. Let's have some fun."

I decided to be indulgent. By this time, our starters had arrived. The tagliatelle smelled so tantalisingly of summer truffle, I was tempted to stick my nose into the plate. Before tucking in, however, I made it clear to Tito that I wasn't available for the kind of 'fun' he obviously had in mind.

I had no interest in getting any more involved in my date's family matters. After twisting the lower half of a colossal pepper mill over my plate, I armed myself with fork and spoon. This was a feast for the palate.

The Argentinean bore his defeat with composure and our evening together turned out to be a very entertaining one. He told me how he had expanded his business over a period of 25 years and had become a millionaire many times over. We discussed old and new marketing methods and he described some of the unconventional advertising measures he had employed.

"I've been talking about myself all the time. Why don't you tell me something about your job, Conny? I read that you used to work with Harald Schmidt. I always liked him. What was it like working with him?"

"It was fun, I really liked working with him. I also learnt a lot from him. He's a brilliant mind, one of the few in the German TV business. I have lots of stories and anecdotes from my time with the Harald Schmidt Show but, unfortunately, I can't tell you about them. They're top secret!"

Tito looked at me with disappointed dachshund eyes.

"One of my favourite sayings from him is: 'When I take a breath, a whole page in a German newspaper analyses the relevance this inhalation for society.' Or: 'I play the part of a TV cruise ship captain out of the deepest conviction that this could be the model of the future:

an ever-aging generation is shipped from A to B for no reason at all.'"

The Argentinian laughed so loudly that the guests at the adjacent table glared at us. I lifted my hand apologetically.

"Conny, it'll be between you and me. Go on, tell me a bit about it."

I looked at Tito with raised eyebrows. Talking of which, I can only raise both eyebrows simultaneously. I have practised in front the mirror for years but I still can't raise just one eyebrow the effortless way French women do it. It's impossible. Once, I even taped over my left eyebrow to try and get used to the position, but I looked like I'd walked headfirst into a door. I'd better forget that idea. I took a deep breath.

"Okay, Tito, sometimes I make up stories just to entertain people, like this one:
      The show was always recorded at 7 pm under live conditions, which means that no changes were made in the cutting room afterwards. Everything was broadcast on television just the way it happened.
      The audience was let into the studio long before recording started, accompanied by the announcement: "Recording will start shortly". If they'd been told they'd be sitting around in a cold TV studio freezing their arses off – excuse my French – for two hours, most of them would probably have left.
      So there they sat, cheerfully expecting the show to kick

off at any moment. Some kept turning around, hoping to get a glimpse of Harald Schmidt, but of course he was still nowhere to be seen. At this point, he was still relaxing in his office, watching the audience over a cup of tea. The studio was fitted with secret cameras, enabling him to see who was in the audience that evening from different angles.

Who looked especially interesting? Who might it be worth talking to – for the sake of viewing quotas? Based on facial expressions, which person was likely to give particularly entertaining answers to his questions?

About half an hour before recording was due to start, a clown would jump out onto the stage. He was desperate to earn some money and game for anything. He entertained the audience with jokes and silly comments and was supposed to warm them up to 'operating temperature', as the presenter called it. Peppo the clown told the audience – who by now were almost frozen to death and incapable of offering any resistance – that they were about to have the experience of their lives.

They believed him.

Peppo then introduced the show band 'The Jingle Bells'. Yes, Harald Schmidt had his own show band. They cost him a fortune every month and performed for an average of two minutes per show. The Jingle Bells came onto stage with their instruments one after the other, doing little dances of joy – unsurprisingly, considering the money they were earning.

Meanwhile, Schmidt, as usual, left his office and shouted his head off backstage, firing himself up for the show. Two interns stood to his left and right, telling him all the time that he was mankind's greatest saviour since Martin Luther King.

The make-up artist would powder Schmidt's face for the tenth time and a third intern pulled up his silk knee socks made by ecologically-bred silk worms. Then he was ready to liberate the audience from their frozen state. All the studio lights flashed on, the Jingle Bells burst into tune and Harald Schmidt leapt onto the stage. The audience went wild and the show could begin. That's what happened every night."

Tito had listened to me attentively and was evidently highly amused.

"Conny, you're a great story-teller, but I'm just wondering now how much of that was true."

All the laughing gave his face an even fresher colour than at the beginning of the evening.

Doublevision is still married and travels the world on business. We never ate out again.

12. Date: MaximeiC

Was my Prince Charming deliberately keeping me waiting until the very end, making me pick up the wrong piece of paper every time? Were the really remarkable men I'd been dating all these months only meant to prepare me for the salvation from singlehood that would be brought to me by Candidate No. 12?

I picked up the piece of paper and slowly unravelled it. Another candidate from France awaited me. One of the sites I'd signed up to apparently cooperated with dating portals abroad, hence the responses from Italy and France.

MaximeiC (49, Virgo, Virgo rising)

The double Virgo and his profile name gave me food for thought. Maxime is the French derivation of the Latin word *maximus* – 'the greatest'. Did his name reflect his nature? He was the only candidate to use his real name as his nickname. This could either mean he was normal, or narcissistic. The photo was of a 1.75-metre-tall, fairly attractive man with the beginnings of a paunch. Dark, shoulder-length curly hair framed a friendly, open-looking face.

Astrologer Merlin spent a few minutes looking at Maxime's photo and horoscope.

"This is a good-looking man who can be very charming. You can give him a calculator straight away because this

Virgo is careful with his money. Relationships might be a difficult topic for him because there's a certain selfishness about him. He's an insecure man with egomaniacal traits. He has Mars in Libra, which makes him seem a bit like a paper tiger – he's not a rugged cowboy. He probably sees his own life as a constant form of improvisation. I'm very curious to see how your meeting goes."

Maxime lived alternately in several places in France. He and his two brothers renovated old houses, which they then sold for a profit. After finishing school, he'd wanted to become an architect, but dropped out of university. In his dating profile, he listed guitar and piano-playing as his hobbies.

As I'd suspected, '1C' meant one child. Maxime had a daughter who he mentioned in one of his messages. Apart from that, he told me little about himself, but he was very enthusiastic about my pictures and blog. He'd obviously googled me. After writing back and forth for a week, he suggested we had dinner together. I was accompanying one of my clients to an art fair in Marseille and as it so happened, Maxime was working on a construction site nearby.

I had never been to Marseille before, so wasn't familiar with the restaurant scene. I asked Maxime to reserve a table in a nice bistro. He wrote back saying he didn't know any restaurants either, suggesting I used a search engine to find a place and book. Momentarily, I considered resuming my search for a desert island rather than a restaurant, but reserved a table in a brasserie after all.

Unfortunately, my taxi driver didn't immediately find the restaurant and took me on a little tour of Marseille. I stayed calm. At least it gave me the chance to see a little more of the city. Arriving ten minutes late, I entered the restaurant to find Maxime already waiting for me.

"Ah, madame, I thought you weren't coming. I've been waiting for you for some time."

"I'm really sorry! The taxi driver is obviously new in town too, but here I am now!"

The brasserie was not very big and the wooden tables with their red-and-white checked tablecloths and the dark brown wooden floor created a simple but cosy atmosphere.

"Is my choice of restaurant okay for you? I really don't know the scene here."

"Yes, it's really nice."

Barely looking at me, he beckoned the waiter and ordered himself a glass of red wine. I had to politely remind him that I too was thirsty.

I took a closer look at the man sitting opposite me. Maxime wore jeans and a grey-and-white striped shirt that had clearly seen better days. His hands were those of a labourer, covered in scratches and calluses. As I studied his face more carefully, I realised this was most definitely not a 49-year-old man. He might have aged well, but I guessed he was well over 50. Once again, I took the bull by the horns:

"Your profile says you're 49, but even without my glasses I can see you passed that age some time ago."

He smiled at me, slightly abashed.

"Mmmm ... yes, you're right. I'm actually 59. The problem was, only women my age were writing to me. It was dreadful. What do I want with women my age? Then a friend of mine suggested I lowered my age. I mean, I don't look nearly 60, do I?"

Even though he might have been right about his appearance, I found the lie outrageous. Women his age were old, but the same evidently didn't apply to him.

"It's really not easy finding a decent woman online. There are so many really awful ones out there. You know, I'm hyperintelligent. I have my standards."

I could hardly believe my ears. Just five minutes after we'd met, he was telling me he was hyperintelligent??

"Finding a woman like you online obviously doesn't happen often. That's why I wrote to you straight away. You appreciate a person like me. I hope you don't mind that I'm hyperintelligent."

I gave him a saccharine smile and shook my head slowly.

"No, it doesn't bother me at all. You know, I'm hyperintelligent too. What's your IQ? Mine's 154, like Sharon Stone's. I once spent an evening with her in Los Angeles. A great woman, we had a lot of fun together."

Maxime's jaw dropped a little and his glass slipped out of his hand. The red wine splashed across the red-and-white tablecloth, quickly turning it red all over. Part of my white silk trousers turned red, Maxime's face was red, and I started to *see* red. The man was ten years older than he'd claimed to be AND on top of that hyperintelligent. A blonde like me found all this too hard to take.

Einstein leaned across the table and used both hands to try and stop the wine from spreading any further. A waiter, who'd seen what had happened, rushed over to us, threw a kitchen towel over the table and a cloth napkin on my trousers. Another waiter snatched the napkin from my knee, grabbed the salt shaker from the table, removed its top and poured the entire contents onto my leg.

There was something so incredibly comical about the whole situation that I started to laugh out loud. Three pairs of male eyes looked at me in total bewilderment. It was like absurd theatre. After what felt like ten minutes, Einstein found his tongue again.

"Conny, je suis très désolé, how clumsy of me! I'm so sorry."

My online dating experiment was finally coming to an end with this dreamboat of a man and I was already looking forward to my forthcoming holiday like an excited child.

In an old manor house near Saint-Rémy-de-Provence, I had rented a small apartment and was planning to travel there directly from Marseille. I didn't give a damn about the man sitting opposite me. It could even have been Quasimodo that I was dining with.

I already saw myself wandering through the streets of Saint-Rémy-de-Provence, searching for spices and oils at the amazing markets of Avignon or Arles, or trying out new recipes in the manor house kitchen. The road to Saint-Rémy-de-Provence is lined with old plane trees, which Vincent van Gogh immortalised in his painting 'Les grands platanes'.

At the end of the road leading into the town is a small, modest-looking brasserie. When I sit there at one of the old wooden tables in the courtyard, a slice of freshly baked quiche on my plate in front of me, taking in the smell of herbs and summer and listening to the leaves in the old plane trees rustle in the breeze, I always feel a little closer to paradise.

I had already left my body. Only an empty shell sat at the table with the now red-stained tablecloth opposite a man with a red face. What was now his fourth glass of wine undoubtedly added to the ruddiness of his complexion. The man clearly drank quickly and copiously.

"No worries, Maxime, it can happen to anybody. Let's find something nice to eat and have a chat."

Einstein told me how much he loved music and what an excellent pianist he was. Unfortunately, circumstances had prevented him from pursuing a career as a professional musician, just as he'd been unable to finish his degree. His daughter, who was the result of a brief relationship with a Spanish woman, was now grown up. He had avoided marriage all his life and none of his relationships had lasted longer than two years. He had nothing nice to say about any of his previous girlfriends. They were either too stupid, too fat, too greedy or too bad in bed.

When he talked, he gesticulated with his hands, but his eyes were empty. There was no warmth in them. He made me shiver.

"I've had a long day and I have a lot of appointments with my client tomorrow. If it's alright with you, I'm going to go back to my hotel now."

"That's fine, madame, you need your beauty sleep. Would you like me to go back with you?"

There was nothing I wanted less than to be accompanied to my hotel by Einstein.

"Thanks, but I'll call a taxi. Shall we pay?"

Maxime beckoned to the waiter and asked for the bill.

"Conny, I was going to offer to pay, but I haven't got much money left. It's probably best if we pay separately."

With no mention of my ruined trousers, he totted up exactly what he owed. I gave the waiter my share, said goodbye and collapsed with relief onto the back seat of the taxi that was already waiting for me outside. I stared at my white silk trousers, which I would probably have to dye red. Despite the salt attack, the red wine stain was still very visible.

That night and the following morning, Einstein sent me the gushiest of messages. He said he was fascinated by the beautiful, successful blonde woman he'd met. He was truly mortified about the matter with the red wine. He really wanted to see me again and treat me to a meal to make up for the bad impression he'd made. The evening hadn't gone well at all.

Fearing that another evening with Maxime would well and truly dampen my spirits, I thanked him but politely turned down his invitation. I wasn't expecting Einstein to react the way he did. He wrote me one message after the next, and called me up and apologised what felt like 100 times. He suggested going to a really excellent restaurant, promising that this time, of course, he would make the reservation. He said he also had another surprise in store for me.

Should I give the candidate another chance? Maybe he really had had a bad evening and I'd been too quick to judge him? Plus, I admit I was curious about the surprise he mentioned. What could it be? A special candlelight dinner on the roof terrace of a restaurant? A private concert on an especially installed piano? He'd described his skills as a pianist in the greatest of detail. I decided to make an effort and accepted his invitation for the following evening.

It was a hot summer day and I'd spent it dashing from one appointment to the next with my client at the fair. By the time I returned to my hotel after nine hours of non-stop meetings, I was completely exhausted. I toyed briefly with the idea of cancelling dinner and just enjoying some peace and quiet. The hotel's beautiful terrace overlooking Marseille's old harbour, the early-evening sunlight, and room service were all too tempting. However, I pulled myself together, jumped in the shower, threw on a summer dress and took a taxi to the address Maxime had sent me.

The restaurant was part of a beautiful hotel, an old mansion in the heart of Marseille which had been very tastefully and carefully restored a few years previously. Arriving punctually this time, I stood and marvelled at the inner courtyard which was lit by torches and candles. Maxime was nowhere to be seen, so I sat down in one of the inviting wicker armchairs and waited. After a few minutes Maxime texted me to say he was on his way and would be arriving soon. After another ten minutes he was still nowhere to be seen, so I ordered a drink from a very charming and attentive waiter. When the young man served me my drink a few minutes later, we started chatting about the history of the building and he obligingly and patiently answered all my questions. Maxime finally arrived almost half an hour late, just as the young waiter and I were laughing loudly about something he'd told me about his life as a waiter.

Einstein evidently didn't find it funny. He greeted me with narrowed eyes and pursed lips.

"What did that man want?"

"That *man* is a waiter in the restaurant. He kept me entertained and brought me a drink while I waited half an hour for you."

"I got stuck in traffic, I'm sorry."

First impressions are sometimes right after all. I thought of the beautiful terrace in front of my hotel room, of the peace and quiet there. Then I thought about my holiday, which would start the next day. I felt the anticipation growing in me. I wanted to get away from all these dating disasters, these bad vibes, lies, these narcissistic men and their pseudo jealousies. I just had to get this one last dinner over with. I tried to blank out Einstein as best I could and enjoy the stunning location. "This really is a beautiful old mansion. I'm curious to see what the restaurant is like inside. Come on, let's go in. I've hardly eaten anything all day."

"What do you think of my surprise?"

I scanned the terrace and then looked at Einstein, slightly mystified. Was there a Tiffany box hidden away somewhere in the courtyard? Or a voucher for a hotel spa treatment? Had I missed something? A little perplexed, I walked around the terrace. "What surprise do you mean? Sorry, but I haven't noticed anything special. Can you give me a clue?"

"I'm wearing a suit. That's my surprise."

I stared in disbelief at his wrinkled, cheap, grey viscose suit and nodded in agreement. "Très chic, Maxime, très chic. Wow, that's really some surprise."

The evening was another disaster, even worse than the first. Einstein jabbered on about all the amazing things he'd done in his life, how many idiots he'd come across, how many dreadful women he'd dated online. Then he showed me a dating app on his phone and the 32 new messages in his inbox.

"All these dull, unattractive women are interested in me."

I hastily ate my meal and continued to dream of Provence. At one point, he stared at me critically.

"Conny, it's great that you're trying to speak French, but you have a very strong German accent. It's really noticeable."

"Of course I have a German accent, but at least I speak some French. Let me hear your German. I'd be interested to hear how that sounds."

Frowning, my date took a large swig of red wine. Needless to say, he couldn't speak a word of German. In front of me sat a man with a severe narcissistic personality disorder. He was the greatest, and everyone around him was a loser. If you told him about something nice or special you'd experienced yourself, he wasn't in the slightest bit interested. He was totally incapable of relating to other people or their needs.

Once again, I feigned tiredness and told him I had to leave.

At the end of our brief evening together, he checked the bill three times and with obvious reluctance placed the money on the table. I ordered a taxi, made it clear to Einstein there would be no more dates and returned to my hotel. Thank God I never heard from him again.

My trip to Provence began the next day. During the short train journey, I sat next to the window and watched as the beautiful countryside passed by. I thought about my dating experiences of the past few months and felt sorry for all the women who'd already had or may still come into contact with these men.

Shortly before the train drew in at Avignon station I gathered my bags, left my compartment and headed towards the exit. In front of the toilet stood an elderly, very elegant looking gentleman wearing a cream-coloured turban and a white linen suit. He had a beautiful bronze skin tone and was obviously of Indian origin. There was something magical, dignified about him – and yet there was also something repulsive about him too. Still wondering what attracted my gaze to the man, but also made me stand back, I noticed yellow and brown stains all over his white suit. Suddenly I realised: the man stank to high heaven – to put it bluntly, of shit!

I was spontaneously reminded of something TV presenter Roger Willemsen once said on a chat show about the time he'd carried a young monkey through the jungle of Borneo:

"All of a sudden, the orangutan opened his rectum and released a bile-coloured liquid that spread across my lap."

There were absolutely no signs of any large animals on the train, and I wondered what on earth could have happened. The Indian man read my mind. Bowing slightly, he said in a deep, sonorous voice:

"Madame, I'm very sorry, but the toilet exploded on me."

My hand groped around for a door handle to steady myself on and I tried to stifle the snorts that were about to escape. In vain. Low wheezing chuckles started to erupt into loud raucous laughter. And the man laughed with me. It was hot, everywhere stank of shit, but we laughed until we cried.

"Madame, I'd love to invite you to join me for a coffee but I simply smell too horrible. What a shame!"

After saying good-bye to each other on the platform, I continued my journey on to Saint-Rémy-de-Provence.

My holiday was a dream. The old restored manor house on a wine-growing estate had four apartments, a large pool and a fully equipped al fresco kitchen in the courtyard. I made friends with the landlords and with guests from all over the world, and occasionally we spent evenings together under the old plane tree around a huge wooden table laden with the most delicious food, Champagne and fine wines.

During the day, I went on trips, wandered across the fields, and enjoyed the chance to relax and unwind. In the village there was an excellent delicatessen. I discovered it by chance one day and stopped in front of the shop window, completely entranced by the food on display. There were delicious cooked dishes, exquisite meats, herbs and spices, sauces, pastries, wine and Champagne. I was in paradise.

And this is how I met Arthur. The third-generation owner of my landlord's large neighbouring vineyard had built up a small delicatessen empire with stores all over France. He lived and managed his business in Paris but regularly visited Provence to check on his vineyard.

We got talking and from then on, I went to his shop almost every day to buy some little delicacy to eat in the evening. Arthur knew my landlords, and a few days after we'd met, he joined me one evening under the old plane tree. We liked each other. Arthur, early forties, tall with light brown curly hair, was an attractive man. Recently divorced, his son lived with his ex-wife in Paris. He spoke affectionately about his son and with great respect about his former wife. I liked that. Like me, he had travelled all over the world, and because he had worked so hard in the last 15 years, his marriage had fallen apart.

On the day of my departure, he accompanied me to the station.

"Come and visit me in Paris."

"I'd like to. I'm there fairly often anyway."

"I'd really like it if we could continue our conversation, Corinne."

Arthur always called me Corinne, the French version of Corinna.

"I'll be in touch the next time I'm in Paris, I promise, Arthur."

We embraced, I got into the train and he waved good-bye. It was like a scene from a film.

As fate would have it, I had a meeting in Paris five weeks later. I sent Arthur a message, telling him when I'd be in the city. He answered immediately and less than an hour later sent me the reservation for a restaurant he knew well. I couldn't open the attachment with the reservation details so asked Arthur to send me the address again, but he had a better idea.

"I'll pick you up at the hotel and we'll walk there together."

It was a rainy morning when I arrived at the Gare du Nord, but I love Paris even in the rain. Arthur apologised profusely for not being able to meet me at the station. He had to check a large Champagne consignment to the US and the plane wouldn't wait until after my arrival. Mon Dieu!

My hotel was in Saint Germain. I love this part of Paris and always stay there whenever I can. The French taxi driver noticed my German accent and on the way to my hotel enthused about the design of German cars.

"Madame, French cars are rubbish. You know, when you close the door of a French car, it goes 'BAFF' and rattles and clanks. But when you close the door of a German car, it goes 'PLUPPP' and that's it!"

As he was talking, he kept pointing scornfully at passing French vehicles, driving even more crazily than the French usually drive. Every time a German car passed he went wild with enthusiasm.

"Madame, Mercedes magnifique, BMW incroyable."

I patted his shoulder from behind and asked him to drop me off alive at my hotel.

Arthur picked me up at the hotel in the early evening and we strolled towards Pont Neuf and from there along the Seine. The weather had changed for the better and it was now a balmy late-summer evening. We sat down on one of the stone benches.

"Maybe I'm imagining it, but the light always seems so special when I'm in Paris. Isn't it beautiful, the atmosphere, the way the evening sun casts a warm light on the bridges over the Seine?"

Arthur nodded.

"You're right. You can just sit here and reflect. Sometimes I come here and just look at the water, it's almost like meditating."

My stomach rumbled and Arthur started laughing.

"I see, Corinne, you haven't eaten anything all day again." I nodded.

"Come on then, let's walk to the restaurant."

When you turn off Rue Dauphine into Rue Christine in Saint Germain, after a few metres it's hard to believe you're in Paris anymore. All is suddenly quiet. On the right is a long row of sandstone-coloured buildings that are lit up in the evenings. There's a small old cinema that shows original versions of classic American movies. The light is wonderfully soft. Located at the far end is a small restaurant named after the street. For many years, this has been one of my favourite restaurants in Paris and, without knowing it, Arthur had reserved a table for us there.

We entered the small lobby and received a warm welcome from the restaurant manager, whom we both knew well.

Arthur and I spent a light, tingly and entertaining evening together and were the last guests to leave the restaurant, well after midnight. Everything felt good and right and I decided to stay.

This was the start of my time in Paris ...

Summary: What Can Be Said About the Emotional Well-Being of Our Society?

Is it worrying that a single woman in her mid-40s only meets such – let's say – remarkable men and has so many bizarre experiences with them?

Do handbags make the better men?

During my online dating phase I met up with far more men than the ones I describe here. With only a few exceptions, these men were clearly insecure, narcissistically inclined individuals, who lied and cheated. In their profile pictures, they presented an image of themselves that was more attractive, smoother and therefore younger than they really were. They lied about their age, kept quiet about families and wives or partners, and fabricated stories about separations and professions. Over two thirds of the men were not interested in a new relationship. All they wanted was to test their market value, boost their egos and have some fun. The men I found myself sitting opposite were often not just insecure but incapable of committing themselves to relationships.

I talked to female friends and acquaintances and learned about the many adventures they'd had in the online dating world. The situation was not much different with my male friends. They talked about 'difficult' women who used dating sites to find a provider, a breadwinner. Three middle-aged couples who had met online did not openly admit to this, but preferred to make up a story. It's evidently still not 'chic' to look for a partner online and actually be honest about it – at least, that's the impression I got from people of my generation.

I dated men, not women, so my accounts and thoughts in this book refer to men only. This shouldn't mislead us into thinking that narcissism is an exclusively male phenomenon, even if more men are affected than women. There are female narcissists too. Anyone who has ever had any dealings with such women will know that it's no fun either. Some men suffer greatly from the narcissistic behaviour of their partner or boss, and, naturally, there are also women who are incapable of committing to relationships.

I had a growing suspicion that both men and women are finding it increasingly difficult to sustain truly meaningful, equitable relationships in which physical, emotional or verbal violence is not the order of the day.

The more intensively I examined the reasons for the success of online dating sites, the more I read literature about narcissism, traumatised people and the generation of war children and 'war grandchildren'.

War grandchildren are the offspring of the children of World War Two, in other words men and women born between 1960 and 1980. I myself am a war grandchild. My parents were war children.

In her book *War Grandchildren – the Heirs of the Forgotten Generation*, Sabine Bode describes how we grandchildren of war have been indirectly traumatised by our parents and by the war traumas they endured and never worked through themselves:

"The legacy of war still impacts many families today, even second and third generations. They lacked nothing. Or did they? [...] Why is it that so many feel they don't really know who they are or where they want to go? What are the underlying reasons for this diffuse fear of the future? Why do so many remain childless? It is still a completely new idea to them that their deep-seated insecurity could come from parents who never processed their own war experiences. Is it possible that a period of time over 60 years ago could have such powerful repercussions on the lives of children born much later?

The so-called 'children of prosperity', as this generation is also known, are heirs not only in a material sense but also an emotional one. Expressed in layman's terms, we too have inherited the experiences and traumas of our parents and grandparents from the two World Wars.

Why are so many men and women of the grandchildren generation plagued all their lives by emotional insecurity and fear, despite having had a good education? Why are they afraid of hardship despite a good income? Why don't they feel truly accepted or loved in their own right? Why do they lack self-confidence or believe they're only entitled to recognition and love if they achieve something? Why do they focus more on outward appearances than on their emotional well-being, suffer burnouts, become depressed, develop addictions and psychosomatic illnesses and often struggle in relationships? Why do they survive rather than thrive in life?

Almost all the men I met during my online dating phase were members of the 'grandchildren generation', in other words, aged between 40 and 60. Almost all of them showed one or more of the above symptoms. In this context, it is irrelevant whether we meet traumatised people online or offline. Either way, without psychological treatment, the symptoms make life difficult for everyone concerned and, above all, cause conflicts and great suffering for the affected person. Later in this summary, my interview partners discuss the characteristics that are typical of people who look for a partner online.

When I examine my own background on the basis of these insights, I can conclude the following:

I am the daughter of an alcoholic. For as long as I can remember, I only ever saw my father in a state of drunkenness. I don't recall him ever uttering a clear sentence. My mother suffered from depression her entire life. In her mid-40s, she was diagnosed with breast cancer, and at the age of 53 she died of it. My mother was born in Vienna where she lived until she was seven. Because of the war, my grandparents were forced to leave Vienna with their daughter more or less overnight, moving to the Rhineland to stay with relatives of my maternal grandmother. Struggling to feed their own family, my grandmother's relatives were less than enthusiastic about the new arrivals from Vienna. Not much later, my grandfather died at the age of 42. My mother, who was very close to her father, was left behind with her increasingly depressive mother, eventually developing depression herself. My grandmother was widowed at 41 and never had a relationship with another man.

As an only child, I began to look after my parents when I was six. I did the shopping and taught myself to cook while my mother was laid up in bed for days with migraines. When my father, who was a construction worker, came home from work in the evenings drunk, I had cooked his meal and made sure my bedroom was clean and tidy. At school, my goal was to achieve top grades with the least amount of effort, and somehow, I managed to do this surprisingly well right up until my *Abitur*. My mother complained to me constantly about my father, and my father did the same about my mother. I was 14 years old when my mother was diagnosed with breast cancer. My childhood – for what it was worth, given my family circumstances – was well and truly over.

I accompanied my mother to hospital for numerous operations, listened to doctors explain the advantages and disadvantages of various types of chemotherapy treatments, and in the evenings tried to explain everything to my father. He was incapable of offering my mother emotional support or making any kind of decision.

When my mother's condition continued to deteriorate, I learned to inject her with morphine every few hours and administer infusions. Our old family doctor called in every day to check on her. I also looked after the household and took my school-leaving exams. I went on to complete a training programme, still looking after my mother and the household. Although the situation at home left me with little time for my education, I finished my course at the top of the class with the highest marks in all ten subjects. I managed to function perfectly without any major disasters, as if I were in a trance.

The day I enrolled at university to take a degree in law, my already frail mother handed me a bouquet of flowers with the words, "I'm giving you flowers now because I won't live to see you graduate." Indeed, she died shortly after. My mother had asked me if she could die at home. She didn't want to go to hospital.

I continued to function after her death, finishing my law degree in the standard study time while working part-time for the local authorities to finance my studies. The day I passed my law exams, I was the only student to stand outside the court building alone, with no family members to congratulate me. When I told my father over the phone that I had passed, his response was, "About time too. You've been a student long enough."

Both my parents used me for their own purposes and abused me emotionally. I simply got on with things, eager to cause as little fuss as possible. I had a roof over my head, clothes to wear, went to grammar school, had a hobby (I sang in a choir for 16 years), had enough to eat. What else should a child expect?

My parents showed me no emotions whatsoever. If I didn't 'function' the way my mother expected me to (because I might have had my own opinion about something), she refused to speak to me for days. Appearances were very important to my parents. Outwardly, everything had to be picture-perfect. After all, what would people, what would the neighbours, say? My father repeatedly told me, "As long as you're under our roof, you'll do as we say."

My father was never aggressive to me and he never hit me. Unlike my mother. I have her to thank for some severe physical beatings, including being hit on the head with a broom handle when I was an infant. During my childhood and teenage years, her emotional abuse sometimes brought me to close to despair.

When I was a teenager, my parents told me I had spent time in a children's home when I was a baby. They had to renovate a new apartment and I had been "in the way". They refused to say more and I had no recollection of that time myself. A while ago, I tried to find out more about my stay in the children's home, but unfortunately, all the documents from those years had been destroyed.

At the age of 18, I discovered that I had a much older brother from my father's first marriage. There had been no mention of his existence before. He played no role in our family life whatsoever. My brother Bernd died suddenly of a heart attack at the age of only 43. Sadly, we never met.

As a child, a teenager and even as a young woman I was unable to make sense of any of this. However at some point, many years after my mother had died, I started to ask myself more and more questions. Why did I work so much and find it so hard to switch off and relax? Why did I always have a problem saying no when things were too much for me? Why was I never at peace with myself or feel like I didn't belong anywhere? It was as though I had no family roots.

Today, I know that both my father and mother, war children, were highly traumatised people and completely overwhelmed with the task of looking after a child. Their own traumas had made them profoundly unhappy and incapable of relating to other people's feelings. From their perspective, they did their best within the realm of their abilities, and I learned to detach myself from them.

Sometimes, I am surprised that my glass has always

been half full and never half empty. I love to laugh and would today claim that my life is about living and thriving, not just surviving. To get this far, however, it has taken a great deal of psychological reflection, courage, determination and energy.

Why am I writing so openly about my own personal story? I want to give others courage. I know a lot of people from my generation grew up in difficult emotional circumstances, even if outwardly everything appeared to be nice and orderly and middle-class. I want to encourage others to look at their own stories, and to work on and reappraise their past. It's worth it.

In her book *The Drama of the Gifted Child*, Alice Miller wrote:

"Probably everybody has a more or less concealed chamber within himself, in which the props of his childhood drama are to be found. Perhaps it is his secret delusion, secret perversion, or quite simply the unmastered aspects of his childhood suffering. The only ones who will certainly gain entrance to it are his children. With them new life comes into this chamber and the drama is continued."

Many people (at least in Europe) are still reluctant to seek psychological help or will openly admit to having had therapy. I would like to encourage this. It is the best thing anyone can do for themselves and it is nothing to be ashamed of. People with mental illness still struggle with being stigmatised even today. Fear of exclusion is an enormous burden. I became aware of this when I worked as a press manager for a group of clinics specialising in psychosomatic illnesses.

For example, how can we have meaningful relationships in the form of life partnerships or friendships if we do not love ourselves? If we're unable to take care of ourselves properly? If we're trapped by fears and insecurities? If we haven't yet understood that social media and selfie mania cannot replace the security of the parental home and the love of a mother or father?

How can we offer our own children or children who are entrusted to us (as teachers or educators) guidance if we are ourselves traumatised and have never reflected on our own feelings and behaviour? When I think about the money and effort we invest in our outward appearance, in expensive cosmetics, surgery and Botox, and just how little is invested in the care of our own mental health, the discrepancy seems so stark.

The men I met through online dating sites made me very thoughtful. This is why I decided to continue my research into mental health and ask several psychologists about the reasons online dating is so popular and find out their views on the emotional welfare of society in general. I was particularly interested in the different perspectives and interpretations of this phenomenon.

In his book *Who Am I in a Traumatised & Traumatising Society*, Dr Franz Ruppert, Professor of Psychology at Munich University of Applied Sciences and psychotherapist, writes about the consequences of lack of self-awareness:

"*The aim of a competitive society, therefore, is to appear as intelligent and rational as possible, so people conceal defects in their psyche and hide psychological errors of performance or judgement, even from themselves [...] As long as almost everybody participates in this game of deception, it works to the motto: 'If you spare me from having to declare my psychological defects I will not reveal what I notice about you either.' Moreover, the more authority and power someone holds, the less the people dependent on him or her dare to voice that which is obvious to everyone: this person has a deep psychological defect and is in desperate need of psychotherappy*" (p. 31)

I paid Professor Ruppert a visit in his Munich practice to find out more about his identity-oriented psychotrauma therapy (IoPT).

Professor Ruppert, do you think online dating attracts narcissistically inclined people?

First of all, we have to be clear about what 'narcissism' actually means. By my definition, 'narcissism' is a trauma survival strategy for the 'trauma of identity'. This means that people who are no longer truly connected to themselves compensate for this by creating an artificial 'identity'. They develop an 'imaginary persona' for themselves s and have no sense of who they really are. They have certain ideas about how they think they should be, so that in the eyes of other people they are someone.

For example, they think they have to be great, they're not al-lowed to make mistakes and have to be superior. A so-called narcissist is then under the illusion he's always better than oth-ers in competitive situations, even if this is not the case at all. This is why narcissists can present themselves on dating sites as being as super and great as they want. Initially, nobody can check what's true and what's not true.

Where does all this come from?

In reality, the narcissist doesn't feel big at all. He feels small, insecure and is ashamed of his own existence. Where does this come from? No one makes the decision to become a narcissist. My belief is that these people were not wanted by their parents from the very beginning. They shouldn't be there. Neither the mother nor the father wanted this child, or any other child. Children are often conceived and born into social settings that are hostile, unfriendly and threatening to them; it doesn't mat-ter if families are rich or poor. These children are not important, and if they want to be there, they have to make themselves useful – first to their parents, then at school and later in eco-nomic life. Their only reason for existing is when they are doing something for others.

Many traumatised parents who had the same experiences as children are unable to act in the interests of their own chil-dren. They place their own trauma survival strategies above the needs of their children and misuse their children to survive. Countless children become victims of their traumatised mother or traumatised father in this way.

Parents who are unable to manage their own lives because of their own psychotraumas, for example, may then cling to their children and find it difficult to let them go their own way. They present their own survival strategies as a form of 'caring for' and 'helping' their children. Parents frequently pass on their traumas in the way they bring up their children. In a traumatised society, children are generally seen as objects of reward and punishment that are available to anyone.

What I refer to as 'trauma of identity' is the implicit feeling of not being wanted by a mother and/or father, or perhaps being the wrong sex in the eyes of parents. As a rule, this results in two extreme possibilities for the person in question. Either they slip into depression and see themselves through the eyes of others and believe they are worthless, or they go to the other extreme of 'narcissism' – when they are ostensibly important, stand above everything else and delude themselves and others that they are important.

Why are people attracted by the internet, in general, and online dating, specifically?

Sadly, for the reasons I've already mentioned, a lot of people today are disconnected from their own emotions, they have little self-awareness. They have no perspectives or goals in life because they feel dependent. They simply go along with what they're told to do. As I've already said, this has to do with the way they grew up. Their parents don't really accept them the way they are.

So people focus not on what's going on in their inner world, according to the principle, "I know who I am and I know what I want", but on trauma survival strategies. One of the survival *strategies is called "I want to experience something" or "Something must happen in the external world", because if they look at what's going on inside themselves, they see only emptiness. By dulling their senses to traumatic experiences, they protect themselves. Otherwise, they feel their trauma – there is a fear of death, overwhelming anger, unbearable pain, the most profound loneliness – which they're unable to deal with.*

So people 'feel' through their experiences of the external world. There has to be 'action'. They want to be recognised, loved and noticed. The internet, of course, is a wonderful way to do this. It also explains the enormous popularity of selfies and social media in general. The desire to be recognised and loved is also perfectly normal. The internet, however, cannot replace the nourishing, satisfying kind of love they didn't receive as a child from their mother or father. For example, children who are packed off to a crèche at an early age think there is something wrong with them.

The internet allows us to have new experiences, communicate with people and develop what we consider to be relationships all the time. So, in effect, the internet is a substitute for the connection many people would normally have with themselves. It helps distract their attention further away from themselves and primarily see if something interesting is happening in the external world, because quite often very little or nothing at all is happening inside these people when they are in trauma-survival mode.

To me, online dating sometimes felt like shopping in a supermarket. People look at what's on the shelves on the left and the right, compare offers and around every corner they might find something better.

That's right. We used to have corner shops that sold just one type of toothpaste and one type of bread. Now, there seem to be 100 different toothpastes and 30 types of bread to choose from. People are naturally curious and think that the more possibilities they have, the better, but we can get very lost in all of this.

Can you say anything about the long-term prospects for people who meet online?

This is difficult to say, because a relationship that starts at an office party can sometimes last a long time, sometimes not so long. However, I think there is a certain saturation effect in online dating, similar to junk food. It's not really satisfying in the long term either. If there's really going to be a change in the way people look for partners and sustain relationships, the causes for their behaviour would have to change. As I said, there would have to be a change in the way we deal with our own traumas, whether these are to do with not being wanted, or not being loved as a child, or with nobody showing any interest in us. Or perhaps they are to do with us being a 'project' of our parents, starting with artificial insemination and birth by Caesarean section and culminating in us getting a university degree.

Unless something changes, there will continue to be a demand for addictive stimuli, and the internet is one of many addictive stimuli. Generally speaking, all forms of addiction come about as a result of trauma. Unless we are really prepared to prevent new traumas from occurring or to resolve existing traumas, there will be no long-term changes in society. Eventually, someone will turn up with a new form of distraction after the old ones have become boring.

Looking at society in general, I've often asked myself whether emotional well-being is something that is actually desired. How many billions in profit would be lost if the population was generally in a healthier emotional state? There would be less 'comfort shopping', fewer luxury purchases, consumer loans, addictions and visits to the doctor, and less medication.

That's true. The leisure industry and our entire economic system are also addictive. This is reflected in our economy which is expected to continue to grow. Growth is an addictive idea. There's never enough, we always want more and more. We're not interested in improving the quality of life any more, it's all about earning even more money.

We can never sit back and think: "I'm full, I've had enough." No, next year turnover has to increase again. And how can we increase turnover? By constantly nurturing and exploiting people's addictive needs and by creating new addictions.

We need an 'evolution of consciousness' to recognise all these things, maybe even a consciousness revolution. People need to become more aware of themselves and realise it's their inner life that determines their outer life. Unless people change their inner life, their emotional life, their outer life will continue as always. One day, we will realise we have ruined everything, including ourselves and our beautiful planet.

After my conversation with Professor Ruppert, I took a contemplative walk along the river Isar in Munich. I started to understand why I had always been instinctively sceptical about online dating and the kind of men who sign up to dating sites. When you have examined your own background, your history and traumatic experiences, a relationship with a man who categorically refuses to reflect upon his own life has little if any chance of working.

In an interview in the magazine *Neon* (edition 12/2014), German TV presenter Roger Willemsen, who sadly died at the age of only 60, commented on the providers of 'efficient' matchmaking as follows:

What rubbish! In the primordial situation of love, you never ask: "Do I select someone or do I let myself be selected?". It's about spontaneity, momentariness, profound emotion. Love develops organically in a vague space where conscious decisions have no role to play. Users of dating sites are basically saying: "Spare me the ones that aren't my type." This is how love becomes synthetic.

Asked for his advice for singles, he answered:

Firstly, don't just look at a screen. You have to be able to react to the outside world. You can't do that if you spend all your time staring at a computer. You have to be bolder about speaking. Many people just need to change their language. For example, they should ask questions that are personal, show a real interest in the other person. They shouldn't be afraid of talking nonsense.

My next interview partner was Dr Manfred Nelting, a specialist for psychotherapeutic medicine and general medicine. In 2004, he and his wife Elke set up *Gezeiten Haus*, which has several clinics all over Germany. He has written and published work on burnout syndrome, depression, life crises and genetic research.

Dr Nelting, are dating sites a playground for narcissists?

When I consider online dating, I see that it is frequently a huge disappointment machine. Strictly speaking, it's not really suited to overt narcissists, unless they want to show off or be admired and can perhaps demean other people on a date, which unburdens narcissists.

The term narcissism refers to what tends to be a one-way street. One person elicits from another person the admiration they need for their own self-esteem. A narcissistically inclined person is not good at empathising with other people and doesn't understand that others have needs too. If a child is emotionally neglected, they have to seek confirmation of their self-worth. The child tries out different things and realises, for example, that they perform particularly well or look good and are admired for this, it boosts their self-esteem. The child learns to take something from others as a form of self-regulation, but this does not last long. This means that later in life, as adults, narcissists constantly try to fill their one-way street with traffic, and this causes profound suffering to those who are the givers. However, it also causes suffering for the narcissists because it's like an addiction: they crave more and more admiration. These are very difficult situations and can lead to an overbearing dominance, and in pathological cases, violence and subjugation. Narcissistic personality disorder, however, is not as often the result of early trauma or self-esteem disorders as narcissism.

Who do you think is most likely to use dating sites?

I think that people who gravitate towards online dating – if they have problems – tend to struggle with self-esteem issues. I'd say a person, who is not overly narcissistic and who has a healthy self-esteem, wants direct contact. A lot of people today use work as an excuse for not being able to meet people. They say they have little opportunity to make potential friends during the day, and in the evening, they're too tired from work to go out. Online dating possibly meets the needs of people who feel insecure in direct social situations. A person who is self-reflective and in good health might work less, and in the free time they gain as a result do something other than online dating.

For thousands of years, people have built relationships in an analogue world, in other words, without the internet. But in just 15 years, many would consider this almost inconceivable without the internet. Can you explain this?

Initially, online dating seems easier than meeting people directly. The idea that algorithms can optimally filter out an appropriate match is somehow appealing. You're introduced to a selection of potential partners and you can make your own choice. It gives you a certain position of power and you can choose what you think is the best option. These are all tempting thoughts, but ultimately this is only on a very superficial level. It doesn't work in the slightest. Algorithms can't find 'the' best partner, because what makes a relationship between two people work is something that remains completely unexplained. Similarities, but also complete opposites, can attract and ulti-

mately lead to a fulfilling relationship. I am not disputing the fact that couples meet online and can have a good relationship. But for me, this is more of a spin-off effect, not a widespread phenomenon. Disappointments dominate.

Usually, we meet one person and not lots of people. We get to know someone, really like him or her and possibly fall in love. We never compare this person to others. We test this person at our own pace, and we may find ourselves in a state of personal excitement. That's the beauty of being in love – the person is simply wonderful! If the relationship doesn't begin with this feeling of resonance, but with a comparison, then we have already placed a heavy burden on this person. This person, if they have been chosen, then has to satisfy our expectations. This makes the process of looking for a partner something that it is not. A relationship that starts online continues as it started – with the idea that there might be something better on the market. People who use online dating due to lack of time have too little analogue life for a relationship to work, because a relationship has to be nurtured. And to do that you need space and time.

Would you say that the internet promotes loneliness?

In the last few years, we have observed a general trend towards individualisation and isolation. There is a decline in all types of emotional bonds, be they bonds with family, friends, religion or neighbours. There is greater individualisation, which means we have to optimise ourselves in order to be seen in society. Consumption is seen as a form of reward. We show off what we have and what we can do. For many, being alone means isolation, and this is intensified by digitalisation. Today, we see that people often prefer online activities to analogue life. The number of hours people sit in front of a screen is increasing constantly. In the US, 8 to 18-year-olds already spend seven hours every day in front of a screen. Online dating and social media are part of these 'screen' sessions.

The invitation to optimise ourselves or even create different identities in virtual worlds means that reality is becoming increasingly removed from the virtual world. Sitting still makes us lazier, fatter and more apathetic. The things people write about themselves or the images they present in the virtual world have little bearing on reality. By misusing media, they inevitably become less attractive, or they become compulsive optimisers who have a breakdown as soon as they get a spot on their face. Online dating is a kind of promise that comes faster than paradise, but the promise is not fulfilled.

How would you generally describe the state of society's mental health?

Looking at it from the point of view of children in Germany, I'd say that around half of these children are doing well, the other half not so well. If a supposedly enlightened and highly developed society has to admit to this, then we are in many respects not a highly developed society at all. There are other societies that are more well-developed – both emotionally and in terms of the survival of relationships.

Around a third of children are resilient. If children have someone who acknowledges and supports them in some way or other, this is enough for these children to develop an inner security. They're even able to interpret adverse circumstances in such a way that they are initially good for them. They are less focused on weaknesses and are therefore more likely to survive difficult situations in life. Traumas have a less profound effect because their genetic makeup contains stress genes which have higher thresholds. These children somehow manage to get through difficult situations, and they do so even with a certain light-heartedness. This group of people, for example, will only show limited interest in online dating because the analogue world, sensory experiences, real encounters with people, are much more exciting. These people are also less susceptible to addictions and less likely to experience burnout. The world needs people like this.

Other children are more sensitive and vulnerable to trauma. If they are nurtured and cared for, however, they can be more creative and greater than all the others. However, in the harsh real world they're often lost. This is why many of these children and later adults become ill and are at far greater risk of burnout or addictions.

Is the generation of war grandchildren incapable of committing to relationships?

In recent years, there has been growing evidence that trauma is passed on epigenetically to children born after the war. Many fathers did not return from the war, or they returned traumatised or psychologically damaged. Because of the role men were typically expected to fulfil at that time, the ones who survived had to function and work.

After the war, a lot of children grew up without fathers because, as I said, they were either absent, they were traumatised or they worked like mad to feed their families. With no men around, it was logical that the relationship between women and children was closer. Naturally, there were a lot of traumatised women too. This explains why so many war children and grandchildren grew up in such an emotionless environment. Nevertheless, the bond between children and their mothers was stronger. They had no way to bond with their fathers.

This was particularly critical for boys of the war grandchildren generation, because mothers were usually overly attached to their sons. The husband was gone, so the son was expected to stay at home. It meant that mothers didn't let go of their sons, and the sons of these mothers were unable to take their place next to their wives or girlfriends. The women married the sons of their mothers rather than independent men. A woman can never solve this problem on her own. The man would have to say, "Mother, thank you for giving birth to me, but now I have a wife/partner". They are rarely brave enough to do this and this often causes problems in relationships.

Many of our all-talk-no-action politicians and corporate leaders are immature men – sons who still act in a juvenile way with their mothers. This is a serious dilemma that is rarely talked about. It means they can't really stand by their wives. All of these problems exist even though there hasn't been a war in western Europe for 70 years. We are only gradually working through these issues and realising how important it is that there is no war. What do we have to do for there to be no more wars? No new traumas?

If we look back at history, we can see that we rarely manage to have no wars for longer than four or five generations. Sadly, the majority of people experienced war within two or three

generations, and then it started all over again. We have to con-
tinue the peace project by overcoming all this self-hatred and
inherent aggression, and as individuals develop new strength
to shape society and create a new, more peace-loving narrative.

Looking at my own background with this knowledge, it would seem that I belong to the one third of children (and later adults) who are resilient. I recall a teacher at the day-care centre I went to while at primary school. Although she had no children of her own, this dedicated, warm-hearted woman created a beautiful, welcoming place for children. We played together, went on trips out in the hills, learned to walk on stilts and did all kinds of other adventurous things – it was like a big family. This was *my* time and it gave me the chance recover a little from the troubles at home. Something else that played an import-ant role in my life was music. I really wanted to learn the piano, but my parents were not receptive to the idea. I was given recorder lessons instead (better than nothing) and at the age of six joined a choir where I sang for 16 years. The choir had very high standards, and we won several national and international competitions. This musical training and the many international concert tours we went on were absolute highlights in my life. At an early age, I learned about different cultures and countries. My passion for travel and interest in different cultures un-doubtedly stem from that time.

The fact that such an immense source of joy – singing and music – will always be associated with one of my most bitter experiences – being abused as a teenager by a choirmaster – has been another challenge in my life.

Thankfully, my apparently well-trained stress genes and counselling have helped me work through this experience and enabled me to enjoy life to the full.

I met Dr Marie-France Hirigoyen in Paris. She studied medicine and victimology in the US and France and works as a psychoanalyst in Paris, specialising in psychological violence, psychoterror and emotional abuse. Over 400,000 copies of her book *Le harcèlement moral* (published in the UK under the title *Stalking the Soul*) have sold in France alone, and it has been translated into over 20 languages.

Dr Hirigoyen, isn't it possible to find partners offline anymore?

I think that our society is doing more and more to make people isolated. When we're young, we meet people at university or when we're training for a job. But when we're older and working, it's more difficult to make friends. In business environments today, there's the added problem that men are afraid of being accused of sexual harassment. Here in Paris, more and more people feel lonely. They have their family and old friends but find it hard to meet new people.

How did we use to do this in our analogue life?

I've been working as a psychologist and psychotherapist for many years, and my impression is that things are getting steadily worse. In the past, people made friends through their hobbies or at dances, for example. They socialised more. Today, we have jobs and go home late, at least in cities like Paris. We work a lot, and if we go out, it's with family or old friends. Unfortunately, the internet doesn't make things easier for us. We're constantly looking at our phones, texting insignificant things. Many find it hard to organise their own lives. A lot of patients tell me this.

Does online dating attract narcissistically inclined people?

Not just narcissistically inclined people, no. We're all becoming more and more narcissistic, society is becoming increasingly narcissistic. Today, for example, if we want to find a good job or a partner, we have to show optimal versions of ourselves. We have to be the best. There is so much competition, we have to permanently optimise ourselves.

I think the world is a really complicated place for men today. For a very long time, men were the head of the family. They were in charge both at home and at work. Today, lots of women work and are well qualified. They want to earn the same as men and they fight for equality. Men feel insecure and are often intimidated. A lot of men who come to my practice are lacking confidence. They're convinced they don't perform well enough or cannot fulfil certain expectations. That used to be different. Just ten or 15 years ago, very few men came to my practice. That's changed completely. Nowadays, men feel lost, and that's because of our society. The pressure on them from all sides to be successful is enormous. Men today are often afraid of women, especially successful, self-confident women. They think they have to do even more to actually impress women.

The reasons why men are drawn to online dating are many and varied. Here's one example: a man is still married but his situation at home has become difficult. He wonders whether he should leave his wife or whether his wife might actually be packing her own bags. Online dating gives people the chance to shop around discretely and check out the market for potential successors. If the situation at home escalates – regardless of who leaves whom – the man already has a new partner lined up. Men don't want to be alone. Women are much better at this and many actually enjoy living on their own.

I think the world in which we live is not an easy one. After the war, we had the reconstruction phase and there was lots of work to do. People could achieve a lot through hard work. It's completely different today. Even if you're a really good student, it doesn't mean you'll find a good job. And those who have a job worry about losing it again. In relationships, a lot of things are uncertain. Everything is changing rapidly and people constantly have to adapt to new situations. Just as they've got used to something, the next new challenge comes along. Attitudes have changed too. It's not so much what you do as what you show that counts. People are no longer simply themselves. They play a role they think others expect them to play.

What stories do you hear about online dating?

A lot, and unfortunately they're rarely good ones. One very successful, charming and smart woman told me about a man she met online. He was a successful businessman and an attractive man, all basically too good to be true. He invited her to spend a weekend with him at the beach. They had a couple of won-

derful, romantic days together. He told her what an amazing woman she was. The nights were exciting and there were lots of subjects they both enjoyed talking about. Really too good to be true. After that weekend, the woman never heard from the man again. He never answered any of her messages, and he gave her no explanation for his behaviour. She was confused and very upset because she liked him a lot. She wondered what she'd done wrong. When we took a closer look at the situation together, we realised that she was obviously intellectually superior to him. At least, that's how the man apparently felt because she had a more senior professional position than him. Unfortunately, this was something she experienced often. She wondered whether she should pretend to be 'less smart' when she met a man for the first time. This is what it has come to! In my opinion, men are far more insecure than women. Women are more willing to try out new things. Men run for cover because they think they're not good enough, and they lose their authenticity towards women.

I have noticed that on dating sites, men who are 60 or over look for younger attractive women with whom they can spend their remaining years. The men tell me this themselves. They have earned good money and can afford a good lifestyle, and their new partners benefit from this. But there are two important points to make here. Firstly, these men don't want 'difficult' discussions with their women. They say they've already been through that with their former wives. Second, their new wife should be willing to look after them in old age.

Is this the road to take? A woman should pretend to be 'less smart' if she wants to meet a new man? In many areas of life, we are still a very long way from achieving true equality for men and women. The list of highest-paid athletes published in 2018 by the US magazine *Forbes* revealed huge differences between male and female athletes. Not a single female athlete made it into the top 100 in the 2018 *Forbes* list. Only one woman, Walmart heiress Alice Walton, ranked among the 20 richest people in the world in 2018 (source: *Forbes*, March 2018). Only 1.2% of German CEOs are women, 95% of CEOs of the world's largest listed companies are men (source: *manager magazin* 12/2018). 15.1% of company founders are women, compared with 84.9% who are men, and women are also paid less. Male company founders interviewed in a study said they had earned an average of €3.4 million, whereas woman had only earned €200,000, source: Federal Association of German Startups, Female Founders Monitor 2018). And so the list goes on. I know, it's boring. None of this is new.

Is it also due to male narcissism that women are denied access to important professional positions and men prefer to be among 'their own kind'? Narcissism is more common among men than women, and narcissistic personality traits benefit professional success. It is a regrettable state of affairs. It should give us pause for thought if the personality profiles of male stock market professionals bear striking similarities to those of criminal psychopaths. Indeed, several attributes are present in both leaders and serious criminals. Superficial charm, inflated self-esteem, manipulativeness, lack of empathy, overestimation of one's capabilities, addictive work behaviour, superficial feelings and the inability to form attachments can all initially benefit a career in business (see Reinhard Haller, *Die Narzissmusfalle,* p. 149 ff.).

Today, we can talk at best about the first tender buds of equality. However, even in this early stage, many men are apparently already confused about how to deal with women. There are so many great, smart, dynamic and empathetic women out there, and many haven't even started to discover their own wonderful potential and all the opportunities that are open to them. Gentlemen, there's no need to be afraid of these women! When it comes down to it, we like you too!

What does astrology have to say about the quirks and oddities of human interaction? I made an appointment to meet astrologer Klaus Zepp in Munich. One of Germany's leading business astrologers, he has had his own practice for over 30 years.

Mr. Zepp, what role does the subject of relationships play in your astro-consulting practice?

Alongside job, finances and health, it's one of the key issues. 90% of the people who consult an astrologer do so at a time of crisis. These crises can occur in every possible area of life. In the area of relationships, which we are talking about here, my many years of professional experience have shown me that people frequently fixate on the subjective expectation that the partner is responsible for their happiness. If I'm not happy, my partner is to blame.

What issues also play a role?

One of the most important things that is expected of a partner is that they should be a secure anchor point in the many possible vicissitudes of life, and particularly, they should offer economic security, true to the motto: together we are strong.

The twelve dates were initially about getting to know someone. What do you think about dates like this from the point of view of an astrologer?

Communication is, of course, a means of overcoming distances between people. It decides whether this gap between me and the other person, between me and the world, can be bridged. Opinions tend to differ greatly on this point, because talking about and sharing experiences, feelings and thoughts is apparently far more important for women than it is for men.

Initially, everyone communicates, even those who say nothing.

A picture is often worth more than a thousand words and it plays an important role on dating sites. In chats, however, men often miss out on a potential partner because they write or speak too briefly and matter-of-factly, or they get to the point too quickly.

What is your opinion about the emotional aspect?

Emotions are something women still consider to be a weak spot among men. Today, there's a lot of talk about emotional

*intelligence. We have come to realise that linear, logical ratio-
nal thinking might be useful in a scientific, technical context.
However, we also see that science and technology can produce
some very toxic side-effects, for example in the form of climate
change, that threaten our existence and our future on Earth.
Incidentally, in Indian astrology, which I also studied, the emotional aspect also plays a very important role in terms of a
person's intellectual capacity. We shouldn't forget that although
we can develop functional know-how and technology with our
intellect, the question of where life comes from and where it is
going, and what holds the world in its innermost form together
cannot be answered without emotional intelligence. Only the
heart can comprehend the things that elude the intellect. Incidentally, brain research has long since acknowledged that our
memories are rooted in our emotional system.*

**How would you now relate what you have just said to as-
trology?**

*Unlike science, astrology is not based on causal thinking, in
other words not on the notion of cause and effect, but on anal-
ogous thinking. For example, the Moon in the sky is what emotions are in the human sphere, and these are as changeable as
the position of the Moon. Within one month the Moon passes
through all twelve signs of the zodiac as it orbits the Earth,
which rotates with the Moon as a satellite around the sun. Depending on the position of the Moon at the time of a person's
birth, this individual will have one or another particular char-
acteristic. A person whose Moon sign is Aries, for example, lives
very much according to the motto "Alone against all", whereas*

if a person's Moon is in Libra, the sign in opposition to Aries, he or she will live according to the motto "Don't leave me alone". People's interpersonal behaviour is influenced in a similar way according to their Moon sign. Knowledge of these relationships makes it possible to accurately describe a person's character and assess how well he or she will complement or clash with a potential partner. In a man's horoscope, the position of the Moon shows which basic qualities he expects of a woman, whereas in a woman's horoscope, the position of the Moon indicates how her emotions manifest themselves and to what extent her own emotionality is defined by her childhood.

Which signs of the zodiac are the best match?

I'm reluctant to answer this stereotypical question, even if it's tempting to give some simple, yet superficial answers. Basically, we all have all twelve signs of the zodiac in our horoscope – so to put it crudely, we can all be obsessive like Scorpio, impatient like Aries, indecisive like Gemini, or self-centred like Leo. However, it's important that we use this precious knowledge not to separate people from each other but to help us understand people as they are. Learning about astrology is like learning the language of the soul. At heart, all of us want to be heard first and, if possible, also understood. Best represented in Greek mythology, this knowledge has for centuries fulfilled its function of articulating the adventures, comedies and tragedies that life offers us, making sense of them for our emotional development and helping those who ask for it overcome crises.

Should we get rid of the internet? No, of course not. The internet and digitalisation have brought many wonderful opportunities for progress in all of our lives. Nevertheless, I am convinced that in certain areas of life, for example, when we are looking for a partner, the internet is of little or no use at all. Or at least, it should be used very prudently and only in moderation. We should treat artificial intelligence with caution, return to a more analogue lifestyle and trust our instincts to guide us and accept that these instincts are indispensable for our coexistence. To achieve this, however, we must have a healthy self-awareness, and trust in ourselves. Hearing, seeing, smelling – all this is what makes face-to-face encounters so wonderful and so unique. Many people have already forgotten how to behave in certain areas of analogue life, for example, they no longer know how to flirt. Instead of going to restaurants on their own in the evenings for a drink or something to eat (where they might have to interact), they prefer to sit at home in front of a screen, exchanging messages with people they have often never set eyes on offline before (and often never will). And yes, Gentlemen, you're still allowed to make compliments. In my opinion, this doesn't constitute sexual harassment. Recently, a man standing next to me at a traffic light suddenly said, "I just have to tell you how great you look in that dress! I hope this isn't too #metoo for you." No, it wasn't! It was simply a lovely compliment! It made me happy, and I thanked the brave man sincerely.

One of the most intelligent people ever to have lived on this planet, Stephen Hawking, considered human behaviour to be the biggest threat, even bigger than the impending environmental disasters. In an interview with the British online newspaper *The Independent*, he described aggression as "human race's biggest failing", which he said threatened to destroy us all. Hawking urged people to be more empathetic, because he said it would bring us together in a peaceful, loving state.

"If you wish to overcome that feeling of isolation and loneliness, I think that your underlying attitude makes a tremendous difference. And approaching others with the thought of compassion in your mind is the best way to do this" – says the Dalai Lama. Reaching out, getting to know ourselves and others – this is what we need to do in the analogue world. For centuries, we managed to do this fairly successfully, without machines, the internet and artificial intelligence.

List of references

Bode, Sabine: Kriegsenkel – Die Erben der vergessenen Generation, Klett-Cotta, Stuttgart 2012

Haller, Reinhard: Die Narzismussmusfalle, Ecowin, Salzburg 2013

Hirigoyen, Marie-France: Die Masken der Niedertracht, dtv, München 2018

Miller, Alice: Das Drama des begabten Kindes und die Suche nach dem wahren Selbst, Suhrkamp Verlag, Frankfurt 1983

Nelting, Manfred: Burn-out – Wenn die Maske zerbricht, Goldmann Verlag, München 2010

Ruppert, Franz: Wer bin ich in einer traumatisierten Gesellschaft, Klett-Cotta, Stuttgart 2018

Acknowledgements

This book would not have been possible without the unconditional support of many wonderful people.

I would like to thank Dr Marie-France Hirigoyen for the valuable and insightful conversations we had together in Paris. You are so good at saying things clearly and directly, and for many years now, you have gone your own way. Bravo!

My thanks also go to Dr Manfred Nelting for our both intensive and instructive talks in Bonn. Anyone who wishes to find out more about the Gezeiten Haus group of clinics can check out the clinic's homepage:

www.gezeitenhaus.de.

Despite his busy schedule, Professor Franz Ruppert always had time to listen to me, and I would like to thank him most sincerely for our interesting talks and the valuable insights I was able to gain through identity-oriented psychotrauma therapy. We face some very great challenges in society today. You can find out more about Professor Ruppert's work on his website:

www.franz-ruppert.de.

I would like to thank Klaus Zepp for his many fascinating astrological conclusions.

Alexandra, Axel and Tobias: thank you for over 35 years of friendship.

My heartfelt thanks to Inka for believing in the project.

Markus has been like a brother to me for over 20 years. I would like to thank him with all my heart.